THE AUT]

Josephine Sellers is a Mother, GrandMother and writer.
She has had careers in the legal profession, art and craft
movement, publishing, and is a Transpersonal Counsellor
specializing in Equine Assisted Psychotherapy.
She runs a Complementary Therapy and Teaching Centre
in Dorset and lives in Somerset with her husband and
extended family and animals.

PARALLEL WORLDS

A Transpersonal Autobiography

Transpersonal titles for Children of all ages:

The Birds Who Flew Beyond Time
The Great Year: Understanding 2012 and Beyond

Wisdom of the Transpersonal Series:

Journey in Depth: A Transpersonal Perspective
Fires of Alchemy: A Transpersonal Viewpoint
Raincloud of Knowable Things: A Transpersonal Handbook
Symptom as Symbol: A Transpersonal Language

For all our titles please go to:

transpersonalbooks.com

PARALLEL WORLDS

A Transpersonal Autobiography

Josephine Sellers

Illustrations by
Lisa Dickinson

Foreword by
Barrie Anson

ARCHIVE
publishing

2012

This book was first published as
The Return
(Wessex Aquarian Publications 1989)
revised and expanded as
The Return of Yesterday's People
(Capall Bann 2002)

This revised and expanded edition by Archive Publishing
includes all of the first and second editions,
with material up to the present day.

www.archivepublishing.co.uk
(Unit 3 Stone Lane Industrial Estate, Wimborne, Dorset, BH21 1HB)

Text © Josephine Sellers
The rights of Josephine Sellers as author have been asserted in accordance
with the Copyright, Designs and Patents Act 1988.

A CIP Record for this book is available from
the British Cataloguing in Publication data office

ISBN 978-1-906289-19-5   Paperback

All rights reserved. Except for brief quotations in critical articles or
reviews, no part of this book may be reproduced in any manner without
the prior written permission of the publisher.

To contact the author, please visit her website
www.JosephineSellers.com

Printed and bound by Lightning Source

DEDICATION

For Brian and our family.

The cover design is taken from an original silk painting, and as
with all the illustrations in this book,
is by Lisa Dickinson

ACKNOWLEDGEMENTS

THANKS to my Daughter Lisa for the book and front cover illustrations, to Michael Berman for the three Shamanic poems. Also to John Lloyd, my Researcher and good friend, who always made sure I kept my feet on the ground, and to the countless other friends and colleagues, mentioned in my story, who gave of their unstinting help and last but not least thanks to Ian Thorp of Archive Publishing for recognising my story as a transpersonal autobiography.

FOREWORD

I was delighted to be given the opportunity to write a few lines about this unusual book. I met the author, Josephine Sellers, many years ago at a talk she was giving about her strange life experiences. Since then I have had many dealings with the Sellers family and we have become good friends. I have followed their adventures with great interest. Their integrity is beyond question. This is important to know because the story that unfolds in this book might be considered, by some, to be unbelievable.

Josephine recounts their tale with frank innocence. Gradually, she and her husband Brian begin to understand the significance of the task they have agreed to undertake. Their initial reluctance, to be swayed by the information 'channelled' to them by Yesterday's People, is understandable. Then, as their difficult circumstances intensify, they need all the help they can get and begin to trust the guidance they received from various ethereal quarters. The lessons they learn apply to us all.

Life is not easy for the Sellers family but I leave Josephine to tell their story.

Barrie Anson
Homoeopath & Author

PREFACE

This book is a true account of the unusual happenings that have occurred in my life and that of my immediate family. Over a long period they interrelated with each other to produce evidence of earth energies, reincarnation, inter dimensional communicated wisdom and the need for the rescue of damaged souls in limbo. I think even the most hardened cynic would find it difficult to scorn or reject the whole of my story. There would seem to be so much to lose and so little to gain by doing so.

A part of this story, and the events it covers, took place in a very old thatched cottage in a Dorset village. Our move to this very particular spot was foretold by a number of independent sources. The purpose behind our return, as it turned out to be, became known to us - but only after many difficulties.

The story also describes my relationship with a Dorset country parson in a life some four hundred years ago. The Reverend William Thomas has much to say that can help us greatly in coping with the pressures and influences of life today and that is one reason why this inter dimensional friendship was re-kindled.

Psychic phenomenan were also experienced when I went to live with my family in other locations in Wessex and I now began to understand that my life, this time around, was about unfinished business from past lives and I appeared to find myself involved in the phenomenon of group reincarnation.

I have met and made many good friends over the period of time when these events took place. Without their support and encouragement this book would not have been written. They have offered me practical assistance and most of all they have worked alongside me as I have tried to unravel the mystery that has unfolded. The experiences, which I and my family have undergone as a result of the events I am going to describe, have sometimes been very hard. Deep discussion and careful examination of the facts, as they were revealed, made it apparent to us all that the events that took place were more than strange coincidences. They hold a deep and universal significance for all of us. I have been able to prove the validity of some of the psychic information received by searching through historic records.

Brushes with the authority of the Church, the Banking System, Legal Profession, Education and Medical Professions are a part of my story of struggle to find personal authenticity. And I offer the suggestion that in the Aquarian Age, each one of us, needs to seek the knowledge of our own reality. It is through this Gnosis that we will be able to cope with the dangerous tendencies and detrimental influences that are beginning to pile up on the horizons of the future as we approach 2012.

Josephine Sellers
Transpersonal Counsellor
October 2011

CONTENTS

PART ONE – INITIATION

Master Dreamer – by Michael Berman

Cat with the all-knowing eyes
Let me attune to your secrets
And take me with you
On one of your dream journeys
Back to the hidden mysteries
People today no longer have time for
The balance that you possess
Can only come from deep understanding

Cat with the all-knowing eyes
Teach me so that I may find what you have
And what I strive to rediscover.

INTRODUCTION

I have been writing my story for the past twenty seven years and this is how it all began:

Today is Friday 16th December 1988 and I am ready to tell my story. It was five years ago on Monday 15th January 1984 that I felt driven to take up pen and paper and begin to record some of the more unusual events that had occurred in my life. I had a feeling around that time that something was about to happen. I knew the past had a bearing upon what was going to happen in the future and I felt an overwhelming need to recall events from childhood that would eventually yield a result as yet unknown. I knew, then, that I wanted the writing to be a piece of work that would help to enlighten and inspire readers, just as many books about the paranormal had inspired me in the past.

I had, at the outset, little doubt in my mind that we all live many lives in different circumstances and different situations. However, my greatest frustration then was my inability to find other people who shared my understanding. The events of the past twenty seven years have confirmed my suspicions and they have given me, I think, sufficient reason now to offer to others evidence which will help them to decide for themselves where the true depth in life lies.

To give the reader an insight into the kind of person I am, and how I think and live, I had best describe couple of events from my childhood that have always remained firmly in my memory and set me upon a life of psychic exploration. The first experience took place when I was about seven years old. One night I awoke from sleep to find the bedroom flooded in lilac and purple light. Alarmed and frightened I screamed out to my parents as I felt sure the electrical sockets in the room must have been faulty. The intensity of the light seemed to me as if it were electrical and charged with brilliant power. My parents rushed up to the room when they heard my screams and, after calming me, assured me that there was not an electrical problem.

In later years they explained that, at that time, I had been having health problems with my ears, nose and throat and that they had asked for absent healing for me from a well-known and powerful healer; absent healing being a process where a healer mentally directs healing energies to a person at distance. Their explanation of my frightening experience was that I had actually been able to see the healing energies surrounding me. I have since come to know that young children are often visually quite psychic until the more material influences of culture and upbringing repress their sensitivity.

It was during this period of my childhood that I very often had the strange feeling of being watched by a clergyman. Such feelings seemed to be an intrusion into the freedom of my childhood. The 'presence' ever watching over me, seemed to encourage me to take care of my behaviour and to develop a powerful conscience. Not so much a guilty conscience as an inner feeling of what seemed to be the right or the wrong thing to do at the time. Further on into my story, the presence of this clergyman unfolds into a strange psychic relationship.

The final deep rooted memory I have of the inner feelings of my childhood is of an incident at about the age of twelve. I seemed to become aware that I had to work hard at my education in order to achieve success as I felt that I had something important to do in my later life. It was difficult then, as it is now, to put these inner instincts or feelings into words, as I had no idea what it was that was so important for me to do. However, I responded to my intuition, and made a quite dramatic advance in my academic work, moving two grades up the school ladder in a three month period – a progress that would normally have taken as much as two years. After that, life became a serious and worldly affair. I gained good results and left school to become a legal secretary in the City of London until I got married at an early age.

Looking back now it is clear that I was tuned into my inner self in those early years and was responding, if unconsciously, to promptings deep within. This generally seems to have been the case throughout my life, to a greater or lesser extent. However, as my tale will relate, I have now learned to become much more aware of these promptings. My reactions are much more conscious and I am actually able to put them to good use. I know now that we are all born with this gift of intuition. This can be of enormous benefit throughout our worldly lives – if only it were recognised in our culture. If this talent could be accepted and encouraged in early childhood and if we, as adults, could refrain from forcing our own beliefs on our children thus allowing them to develop their own sensitivity, much sadness could be avoided in later life.

CHAPTER ONE

My husband Brian and I met as teenagers and married at a young age on the 3rd September in 1965. He was my one and only serious boyfriend. I saw Brian one evening across a crowded dance floor and an electric current passed from my eyes to his. We have been together ever since. During the years of our developing relationship we rarely discussed anything to do with psychic matters, though he was aware of my parents' interest in the subject. My Mother and Father were both interested in Spiritualism and Spiritual Healing in particular. He does not remember any particularly strange or psychic experiences from his childhood but always had a deep inner conviction of right and wrong. As for myself, during my teenage years, I was more concerned with enjoying life, and since the spontaneous psychic happenings of my early years, I had not experienced anything out of the ordinary.

It was during the early days of our marriage that I began to have memories of what I eventually realised related to a previous existence. These memories were of a grand lifestyle in sharp contrast to the small house and few possessions of our first struggling years. I could recall myself as a young lady dressed in long elegant clothes with long and beautifully coiffured hair. I lived in a grand country house, and I remember waking up in a four poster bed, with breakfast brought to me on a silver tray. From the casement window I could see a beautiful garden in which I would sometimes ride in a horse-drawn carriage. I could recollect instructing somebody to have my grey horse saddled ready for me to ride. In our somewhat austere early marriage surroundings I used to tease Brian by saying I was used to a far grander lifestyle than he could provide for me.

It was not until after the birth of our first child, a girl, Lisa, that I suddenly became interested in exploring psychic phenomena. I felt very much that I would like to visit a psychic medium to see what I might learn. I asked Brian if he would come with me and he agreed, though he admitted that he did not think much of such people. With the help of my parents it was not difficult to track down and make an appointment with a very well know international medium. His performance certainly lived up to his celebrated reputation. He startled us with the highly accurate and detailed psychic information that he received about both of us, past and present. This information was of a personal nature and nobody but Brian and I could have known about it. We were also given a forecast of our future together.

At the time of our visit Brian and I were living at Uxbridge, just outside London. The medium told us of a move, in future years, to a county with a coastal border. A good part of Brian's working life, he said, would be spent designing at a drawing board. Brian was told that he would become well known for the work he carried out and that one day we would own undulating land of a considerable acreage in this coastal county. This forecast for the future seemed most unlikely to us. Brian was at that time working in an office carrying out clerical work and the idea of doing work of a remotely artistic nature had not entered his mind, nor did he consider that he had any such abilities and so we felt this information was possibly inaccurate. It was put to the back of our minds and it was only many years later that we were to realise its startling accuracy.

He also told us that we were soul mates and had deliberately chosen to return together to earth to share our lives for a particular reason. The reason was not given. Over the following years this was something that many mediums told us, although none could, or would, tell us the purpose of this return. I suppose that was for us to discover through inner search.

After this visit, I decided to tell Brian's Mother where we had been. I suppose I expected her to be rather shocked and was very taken aback myself when she replied that she and her sisters had been having psychic experiences for many years. It was a situation she had kept very much to herself, so much so that even her own son was unaware of it. She had a tendency to foresee future events, an ability which she found at times disturbing. She would see, or sense, a disaster and the form it would take but had little idea of when or where it would happen, or the people who would be involved. Brian had never thought very much of psychic mediums. Their failures always seemed more obvious than their successes but much of his scepticism vanished after our visit to this medium and his interest was greatly aroused. From that day on we began to take a far greater interest in spiritual matters and I, in particular, began to read the first of many books in my search for the truth. Through this interest we have met many people who have been strongly gifted with psychic abilities and I became particularly interested in the gift of healing.

Throughout my childhood I had received healing, either by contact, in which the healer actually lays hands on the patient, or by absent healing, when the healing process is projected, as it were, over long distances to the subject. I always found that the contact healing given to me in childhood made me feel very warm, happy and sleepy. One very rewarding experience occurred when I asked for absent healing from an internationally known spiritual healer, Harry Edwards, on behalf of a very dear, life-long, friend of mine who had suffered a severe mental breakdown. Within a few days the results were dramatic. She was released from a mental hospital, having, only seven days prior been committed for a three month stay. She told me, sometime later, that she had sat on her bed one evening, in that hospital, looked at all the troubled patients around her and knew immediately she did not belong with them. From that time on her mental state became totally stable and has remained so ever since. I have to believe that directing healing energy towards her had achieved the desired result, as she had been in a disturbed state for a considerable time. The confidence I gained from this experience led me to seek absent and, sometimes, contact healing for a number of friends over the following years with very happy results.

Two years after the birth of our daughter, our second child was born, this time a boy, Paul. Eight months before he was born I had been told by another medium that my baby was a boy and I was given the exact day and hour of his birth which subsequently proved to be totally accurate.

Despite appearances it seems that every birth is a carefully planned event. I now understand that a soul who is returning to an Earth life selects the circumstances of birth, so that it may embark upon areas of human experience which have not yet been undertaken. This idea of the development of the soul is very ancient indeed and lies behind many of the Eastern religions. As a philosophy, or an understanding, it certainly does help people to come to terms with the tragedies of this life. If we accept, for instance, that people born into terribly crippled bodies or minds may have actually selected those lives for themselves, we would find it very much easier to help them overcome their afflictions and also to relate to them as personalities. Our approach would not be crippled by maudlin and confused sentiments of pity or reproach, nor would we need to blame God every time something goes wrong!

There is much evidence available today to support the theory of reincarnation and I have met many people with their own stories and experiences and they have helped me to find some comfort with my own understandings. However, it is clear to me now that the conflict between my cultural and religious education and my inner knowing continued to cause me discomfort and uncertainty for many years to follow.

Planetary situations at the time of birth play a major part in determining the life experience patterns to follow. The day, date and time of birth are important factors taken into consideration by a returning soul. The predicted arrival of our son emphasized the feasibility of such ideas.

It was soon after our son's birth that Brian began to feel very restless in his office environment. He gave his circumstances much thought and then, one day, announced that he was going to leave the indoor office life behind and become a landscape gardener. Our respective parents were surprised and concerned but my own reactions were closer to astonishment and alarm. We had two young children and a mortgage to cope with and this announcement posed a severe threat to our financial future. However, he obviously had not made his decision lightly and, though he had absolutely no training whatsoever, his mind was made up. I knew he had a great dislike for working inside and I also knew he wanted to work for himself and feel free. Who was I to stop him?

Our first winter was a lean one. We could afford no luxuries; every penny spent was counted. We invested, for us, a small fortune on tools and advertisements. The initial orders were not promising and Brian, working outside for the first time in his life, suffered so badly from bronchitis that the doctor feared pleurisy was on the way. This would return each winter, he assured us, if Brian continued to work outside. Fortunately we decided to ignore his advice but they were worrying times.

I think that, in our inner hearts, we truly felt that we were on the right track and an obstacle was something that just had to be overcome. To others, at the time, and maybe even to ourselves, we probably appeared to be just plain obstinate. We often made mistakes and some of them were very painful but the rewards were a growing strength and confidence.

It was at this time that both of our sets of parents retired and decided to move Poole in Dorset. Not long after they had all settled into their new homes we joined them for a holiday. It took only two such holiday visits to Dorset for Brian and I to realise that Dorset was where we wanted to bring up our children. Once we had enjoyed the delights of the rolling hills and seen the beauty of the Dorset coast line, the London suburbs suddenly seemed very undesirable.

To uproot from London meant having to leave the newly developed landscaping business behind. But, the pull of Dorset was irresistible and by this time we were becoming used to taking risks based upon a gut instinct. Brian reckoned that if he could start up a business once, he could do it again. It was at this time that we recalled the forecast of the well known medium, some four years before. Brian was working in landscape design, and here we were, thinking of moving to a coastal county. In case there may be sceptics who think we moved because the medium said we would, I would urge them to think a little deeper. Would you uproot everything and move to another part of the country, simply because somebody had predicted that you would do so?

We sold our London house, bought a new house on the outskirts of Poole and Brian set to work to re-build his business. The first six months were financially tight. It as an anxious time and we were both a little frightened at the big step we had made.

CHAPTER TWO

Living in Dorset, to us, was a great delight. Our children loved being so close to the sea and we all enjoyed excursions to explore the unspoilt areas of coastline and countryside. It was such a contrast to our environment in London and such a welcome change.

For the first six months after our arrival we focused all our energy on the re-development of Brian's business and on getting our home together. After that we had time to pursue our psychic interests. It was not difficult for us to make contact with likeminded people and we were soon introduced to a local medium, with a very good reputation for her ability to communicate through trance mediumship.

We invited Mrs. Mills to spend an evening with us and, as we had never watched a medium work at a trance level before, we were most interested in what went on. She was a very friendly, jolly lady and we had a long and fascinating discussion about the whole art of mediumship before she got down to work. After a few minutes of silence she slipped gently into a trance state. As she began to speak we noticed that her voice had dropped considerably in tone and had assumed, not only a masculine quality, but a suggestion of a foreign accent. When we questioned her later she explained that the guide who worked through her was an ancient Egyptian. I should just explain here that, usually, psychic mediums work with one or more particular guides and will communication with the guide at a mental or inner level, interpreting and passing on information while in a conscious state. In the case of trance mediumship, the guide actually uses the voice box of the medium in a direct voice communication. Brian and I were quite astonished at the accuracy of the information about the past and present coming to us, through Mrs. Mills. We had, at the beginning of the evening, only discussed generalities. Our policy, when working with a medium, has always been to give away as little as possible about ourselves. Only then can we assess the value of the information received. The material given was extremely personal to us. However, what was convincing was that the guide was able to tell us 'how we ticked'. In other words, the information was more spiritually based and concerned with our perception of life from an inward point of view.

During the course of the session she began to describe, in great detail, an old thatched cottage in Dorset to which, she said, we would one day move. We were given a description of the cottage and the one particular point that has always remained in our minds was that she told us we would be able to sit upon a little window seat, built into the wall of the cottage and look across a rose bed just outside the window to see a bird bath set in a lawn. She said that when we could see this we would know we were in the right cottage. We did not know quite what to think about this information as we had only been in our new home for such a short while and were very happy there. We assumed that this was something that would, maybe, take place much later in our lives. It had been a very interesting evening and we had been impressed with the quality achieved through trance mediumship. We would now have to sit back and let the years pass to see if we would ever find that cottage.

Brian continued to work hard at his business whilst I cared for the children now aged six and four. Every moment of our spare time, however, was spent outside exploring and enjoying Dorset.

In 1973, as our son began to approach school age, I knew that for the first time in seven years knew I would have time to myself. I had no wish to return to secretarial work again and as I very much wanted to work and yet still remain at home when the children were around, I began to think out the best way of having my cake and eating it.

Although I can far more easily accept an inspired thought today, and act upon it, a few years ago I had no such confidence. But, one day, I awoke and knew I wanted to work with dried flowers and, more particularly, I wanted to produce collages with them. I had no idea how to get started. All I seemed to have within me, was a love of flowers and colour which I assume came from my upbringing as a child within the florist trade. My Mother and Grandparents were all florists. This was not quite the same as working with dried flowers and I had no idea whether or not I had any artistic leanings.

Before I could start to produce collages, I had to locate some dried flowers. This was not so easy years ago, as they were not as popular then as they are now. However, Brian made some enquiries through his trade and I ended up with an introduction to an elderly lady who had spent many years growing and preserving garden flowers in Dorset. She had now decided to retire and was in the process of winding up her business. I wrote a letter to her and, in return, was invited to go and meet her.

On that first meeting I felt totally lost and inadequate when confronted with her knowledge and skill. The flowers she had grown and preserved were magnificent. I could not believe such beautiful specimens existed. But I felt myself charged with enthusiasm at what I could see and I must say that her example was the driving force and inspiration behind my floral work as it developed over the years. The generous way in which she passed on her knowledge to me and the close interest she always took in my progress helped to cement a friendship I shall always treasure.

Brian had given me fifty pounds. If he had given me five hundred pounds it would not have been enough. I wanted to buy everything in sight. Eventually I arrived home with my raw materials, bought some hessian, board and glue, stripped out the spare bedroom, set up a work bench and I was ready to start.

My progress was so slow, it took me weeks to develop a feel and an eye for what I knew I wanted to create. But, gradually it started to happen and apart from the enormous worldly satisfaction I gained from producing something that pleased my eye, the inner satisfaction and pleasure was beyond description. I seemed to have opened my mind to a different dimension of thought and I felt as if I was coming alive. I can see, now, that I was beginning to open up the creative side of my personality, a side we all, sadly, too often neglect.

Soon I had produced some satisfactory results and was convinced I wanted to continue the collage work. It became obvious that, if I was to master the art completely, I would have to grow the flowers and preserve them myself. I paid another visit to my flower lady who was able to advise me as to the best varieties to grow and, most important of all, was able to pass on to me many of her secrets regarding the art of perfect preservation.

The months passed and, as I was developing my floral abilities, other areas of our life were also beginning to show signs of movement. Brian and I had been exploring Dorset pretty thoroughly and we were beginning to feel that we would prefer to live in a more rural and isolated environment. Life on a new housing estate had certain disadvantages for the children. In such close communities young children often want to be out and playing with one another seven days of the week. It is difficult to maintain a degree of supervision, or home discipline, when they are living in a lively 'gang' society which sometimes lays too much stress on imitation. Consequently, we felt a more self-sufficient family environment would be better for them. We were ourselves also starting to find estate life claustrophobic, especially after returning from our rural explorations.

We began to look for a new home in the country area a few miles inland from Poole. One evening, after several weeks of searching without success, we saw a thatched cottage advertised in the local paper just a few miles away near Wimborne. We were very tempted to go and view it but decided against it as we were a little worried about the expense involved in the upkeep of the thatched roof. It was also not in an area that particularly appealed to us. The paper got thrown away and the idea put out of our minds. However, several days later whilst I was preparing the evening meal, I got the most overpowering urge to retrieve the newspaper from the dustbin. Rummaging around in all the rubbish I eventually found it and, there and then, rang the estate agent for an appointment to view the cottage. Something had prodded and pushed me. I had responded and two days later Brian and I were on our way to view the cottage.

CHAPTER THREE

We approached up a long and winding, tree-lined driveway which opened into a horseshoe shaped garden with a thatched and white-washed cottage standing right in the middle. It was so quaint – just like having stepped back into the past. We were greeted at the very low front door by a friendly, elderly lady who invited us inside. What a warm atmosphere we encountered as we stepped inside! Brian and I both had the strangest feeling flood through us. If felt as if we had come home. We had returned! This is the only possible way to describe the strange sensation we both felt as we walked through the low front door into the hallway of that ancient cottage. Our hostess led us through into her dining room and there was the little window seat built into the wall of the cottage. Through the window we could see across the rose bed to the bird bath set in the front lawn. The exact description we had been given by that ancient Egyptian guide speaking through Mrs. Mills.

From the dining room we were shown around the rest of the cottage with its low beamed ceilings and sloping bedroom floors. It was a classical English cottage and Brian and I had fallen in love with it. To the front was a pretty garden, with an enormous and ancient pear tree in the middle, whilst the remainder was set out to rows of vegetables and fruit cages. A natural hedge enclosed the garden and beyond it, as far as we could see, were farm fields. It was a truly idyllic environment – just what we had been looking for. The owner took us back inside, sat us down and made a pot of tea. We told her wanted to buy the cottage but explained that we had first to sell our house which we would put on the market immediately. We agreed to pay the price she was asking and our offer was accepted. As she was in no great rush to sell, she was prepared to wait until we could find a buyer for our house. It was clear that she was very fond of the cottage herself and she was only leaving because it was becoming too big a task for her to manage alone. It was important to her that the new owners should appreciate the cottage and would want to go on caring for it as she had done.

It was time to get out of the armchairs and leave. We felt slightly uncomfortable to be sitting in this lady's home, whom we had only just met, but it was the most difficult task to lift ourselves out of those chairs and go. We both felt we wanted to stay and, as we eventually drove away down the long and winding driveway, we were very determined to take ownership of that cottage as soon as possible.

It was August 1973 when we found the cottage and it took us until February of the following year to find a buyer for our house. Those six months seemed endless as we so wanted to get to that cottage. Eventually we were on our way. At the beginning of May we changed homes, just in time for me to plant out the first crop of flowers that I had grown in seed trays in the garden of our home in Poole. The cottage had an acre of garden and I was in a hurry to put it to good use.

Our feelings on arriving to live at the cottage can never be forgotten. The sun shone brightly on that May day. The garden was in a very natural state. Bluebells and Daffodils grew at random from the banks and lawns. Azaleas and Rhododendrons were in full bloom and the fruit trees were covered in blossom. It seemed like paradise to us and such a welcome change after living on a noisy modern housing estate.

Just one week after moving in we invited the medium, Mrs. Mills, who had described the cottage in such detail some two years prior, to visit us and celebrate with a bottle of champagne. We all toasted the cottage, standing beneath the magnificent limbs of the huge Pear tree set in the front lawn. She asked if she could attempt further trance communication work for us and we agreed. Her guide said that we would be carrying out major structural alterations to the cottage over the coming years and we were told that, because of what we would achieve whilst living there, we would, one day, as a result, travel around the world to meet other people in some similar connection. What exactly we were going to achieve was not indicated. We were also told that, as the years passed by, we would gradually take control of the fields around the cottage because of a connection we would

have with horses.

Those early days in the cottage were so enjoyable, full of fun and hope. Yet, all the time the future was slightly tinged with financial anxiety. We had taken on a considerable commitment with the move and our security was very much dependent upon Brian's fluctuating work load. There were times when I felt very insecure and, as I knew I could not bear to have to leave the cottage and its surroundings, I suppose the insecurity was also tinged with fear. But, we had to maintain faith in our intuition and our long term future. Success had been predicted. This cottage had been described to us in great detail prior to our finding it and here we were now – living in it. These facts served to pull Brian and me through some very difficult business and financial difficulties over the following years and helped to give us the courage to persevere when the odds were stacked heavily against us.

At first the children missed their friends and found it difficult to depend on one another for both companionship and play. However, they adapted in time and now, when they look back on their child-hood days, they can see how life at the cottage had such a strong influence on their upbringing. Their thoughts, their view of the world and the people in it, their perceptions of the past and the future were all strongly influenced by the peaceful atmosphere of our cottage near Wimborne.

Not long after our arrival at the cottage we began to feel the need to acquire more animals. We had arrived, on that first day, with just one cat. First of all came a beautiful Old English Sheep Dog, called Samuel, then another one, called Benjamin, arrived to keep him company. We were given another cat and collected several rabbits and guinea pigs. Eventually we ended up with three beautiful horses that arrived at two-yearly intervals and then, to complete the forecast of a few years prior, we took over the grazing tenancies on the adjoining land.

There can be no doubt that the presence of all those animals gave to us a quality of life that must surely be missing when animals are absent. Because of the experience of living with them all, I could not imagine any part of the rest of my life being complete without sharing a home with them. They have so much to offer that brings quality to human life and they are a magnificent way to teach children gentleness and a sense of responsibility.

CHAPTER FOUR

We had not been living at the cottage for very long before Brian and I began to experience a rather strange phenomenon. It was something that remained with us all the years we were there and, as our son grew older, it started to affect him as well. We found that when we travelled a few miles away from the cottage, after a short while we would experience a pulling sensation in the solar plexus. It was accompanied by an overwhelming desire to return home. I would find myself driving home at a ridiculous pace and I would have to force myself to reduce speed. However, we did find that if we travelled a considerable distance away, say over twenty five miles or so, the sensation disappeared and would occur again when back inside the twenty five mile radius. Later, in these pages, I will explore these sensations, for they were no coincidences.

During the first five or six years of living in the cottage we came into contact with many mediums and people who were psychically gifted in many ways. The reader may be surprised to know that, nowadays, there are a great number of people in our society who experience psychic phenomena and there is no longer any reason for anyone who has these talents or skills to feel alone.

All the mediums with whom we had contact, whether they came to the cottage or if we met them elsewhere, kept giving very similar information to us about something we were going to achieve whilst living there. Some felt we were going to own some of the surrounding fields and use them for a purpose. We were told of large number of visitors coming to the cottage in the future and wheelchairs and disabled people were mentioned.

There was most certainly a degree of continuity in each piece of information we received. As the years, and my story, progress it is clear that our interpretation of the predictions of some of the mediums was not always accurate. As a result we sometimes experienced considerable frustration, confusion and unhappiness and it was not until I learned to work at a far deeper psychic level myself that the way ahead became clearer.

I had continued to work at the development of my dried flower collages since our arrival at the cottage. Harvests of flowers from the garden were prolific and the output of collages soon made it necessary for me to find a sales outlet. In the early stages I took my wares to craft shows and to the local markets to sell to the tourists. But I soon tired of having to travel to different towns every day and thought how nice it would be if I could sell direct from the cottage. I applied to the Local Planning Authority to run a Cottage Industry, with a small shop in the garden, and was granted three years of temporary planning. We put up an attractive chalet in the garden and from this little shop, surrounded by the flower beds which contained the next year's raw materials, I sold my dried flower collages and arrangements.

It was as people started to come and look at my shop, that I became aware that the environment of the cottage and its garden had an effect upon them. So many remarked that, when they walked up our long and winding driveway, they felt they were entering a different world. Many begged to be allowed to linger because of the peace they felt there and many returned, time and time again, to enjoy the sensation. It was because of this that Brian and I began to feel that there was something unique about this small area of land upon which we lived. People in general were drawn towards it. Friends who came to stay said they went home feeling charged and refreshed and, on top of it all, there was that strange magnetic pull we both felt when we were away from home.

Brian and I tried to put two and two together. We had been told we were to take control or possibly own, the adjoining land. We were, in fact, already in control of it through our grazing tenancies and so we began to imagine what we would do with it if, by some miracle, we one day had enough money to buy it. The only way we felt able to make use of the additional land would be to extend the very beautiful garden that Brian had made already. We went as far as contacting the owner of the land with a view to a possible purchase.

Our requests were always rejected and we learned that the owner would only sell when he was good and ready and even then at the highest possible price for housing development. Sadly, we were not surprised. The developers were already eating into Dorset and it was only a matter of time before their machines would be chewing away at our own ancient farm land.

For three years I ran my cottage industry on a temporary planning basis. Then the time arrived when we either had to renew it or expand and apply for full planning. With faith in our future we applied to considerably increase the scale of the venture and, once again, our application was successful. We would now be allowed to build a far larger shop and I could invite other craftsmen and women to sell and work with me. However, at this stage we did not have enough money and, for the time being, I would have to continue to work alone in the hope that, one day, I might be able to expand.

Meanwhile my psychic life was not being neglected. There are today, many groups of people who get together to develop their psychic talents. Usually these development circles are run by an accomplished medium teaching and advising the other members. The aim of these groups is not so much to produce more mediums, but to help those many, many people who have undoubted psychic talent which needs to be developed for their own peace of mind or to take care of their own physical health. If all goes well, a receptive person, whose intuitive processes are finely tuned, will not require the services of a medium to interpret them.

One such development circle was quite nearby. I joined it and learned a great deal that helped me to come to terms with my own psychic energy. All the members began to improve over the course of several months and information began coming through to several of them that directly related to our adventure at the cottage. I must stress that none of the members had been to the cottage, or knew anything about it.

The information they kept receiving appeared to come from a little old man who said that he had once lived at the cottage. He kept trying to tell me that there was something of great value buried at the cottage. He also appeared, visually, to a psychic friend of ours who was visiting us and, once again, he passed on the same message.

Buried treasure! Brian and I were more than intrigued by this news which surfaced, again and again, over the next few years and which was going to cause us great confusion and frustration.

Our first reaction was to start digging.

'But where on earth do we start?' I asked Brian

'Well, where do you think he would have buried it, outside or inside?'

It had not even occurred to me that it might be inside.

'There are no foundations, these stone slabs are just laid on the original earth floor and this is the only ground floor room of the original cottage.'

'Yes, but we can't dig up our dining room floor, just like that!'

'Why not?' replied Brian, 'if we try outside it might be anywhere. If we try inside, this is the only place it could be. Anyway, if it rains we can go on digging.'

It occurred to me that there were not many people who had the privilege of being able to dig up their dining room. So we dug it up.

First we removed the stone slabs that covered the old earthen floor. We then piled the furniture and the animals around the sides of the room and set to work. The children joined in, with unusual enthusiasm and as Brian remarked:

'It's not often you get the chance to pull down the family home. Most parents resent even a broken teacup!'

By tea time we had a sizeable hole in the middle of the floor, the furniture and the animals were beginning to disappear behind mounds of earth. But we ploughed on furiously, ever urged by the seductive beeping of a metal detector we had borrowed. Alas for the Siren's song! All that came to the surface were huge chunks of ironstone, probably used as foundations for the ancient mud walls. We had our tea sitting on top of the dining room table, which was perched precariously on the edge of the crater. While we ate the dogs, cats and children happily played away in the gaping mess.

And then to our horror we saw that the hole was steadily filling up with water! Frantically we worked to fill it in. It was with no great confidence that we eventually laid the flagstones back in their proper place. For some time we feared that the monster beneath the house had been liberated but, as the days passed, there was no sign of nastiness creeping up between the stones and life resumed its normal course. At least, the children and the animals had had a wonderful day, but the enigma was going to remain with us for quite some time before we eventually solved it.

CHAPTER FIVE

In the Autumn of 1982 a very good friend of mine gave me the name of a medium new to the area, now working in Bournemouth. This friend, himself, was a most capable medium but he had seen this lady working in public and was impressed by her. I took the name and address and put it to one side thinking I might well contact her, one day, when the time felt right. Some nine months later I telephoned and made an appointment to see her.

It was a hot and sunny early summer's day. The door to the flat was opened by a bright and breezy lady who introduced herself as Eve and invited me inside. I was taken into a room full of house plants and with rows and rows of books upon shelves. The windows were wide open and there was a continuous roar of heavy traffic from the main road below. Eve was very friendly and relaxed. I was invited to find a comfortable seat and instructed not to tell her anything about myself before she started to work, psychically, for me. At this stage she did not even know my name. Eve offered to made a tape recording of our meeting as she felt sure I would not be able to remember everything that I might be told. I was impressed by her approach and felt confident that the meeting was going to be fruitful.

My experiences with mediums have always been positive and I suspect that this is because my own psychic energy reacts strongly with that of the medium and invariably produces a result. But, some people are disillusioned and this can be for a variety of reasons. For a start, their attitude may be negative and this can affect the performance of a medium. For we are dealing now not with the comfortable scientific world of cause and effect but one in which our deep feelings can quite unconsciously wield the energy of a powerful generator. Or it may just be a case of the medium not being particularly efficient or confident. But most people who are looking for a service will first look for somebody who has a good reputation. The same applies to mediums and I would say to those who want to make contact with one to ask around first, before making your appointment.

As I had anticipated with Eve, the quality of information given was excellent. I was immediately told of my connection and work with flowers. A detailed physical and personal description was given of my deceased grandFather with information about his business connections within the florist trade. I was told that my floral work was being influenced by a young Japanese lady, who had been around me for many years. This was remarkable news because, as a young child, a contact healer had once told me of a Japanese girl, called Crystal Clear, who was close to me. She also gave me a pastel sketch of this girl which my Mother had kept. It did not surprise me at all to be told that there was an external influence behind my floral work. In fact, long ago I had come to a similar conclusion. This Japanese girl told me, through Eve, that to me my flowers were 'a way of religion'. If she meant this to mean that they brought me closer to my Creator and my origins, then she was correct. I was told that the essence of my floral collages acted as healing therapy to those who bought them. I have since come to understand more fully what this means.

Since thought contains energy, in the same way that any other action does, then the care that goes into a creation is part of the energy of that creation. From the actual growing of a flower from seed, to the finished, designed and arranged collage, the energy of care and thought has gone into every stage. My thoughts are contained within the finished creation and the energy from it benefits those who are capable of absorbing those 'vibrations'. This principle, of course, applies to any creation. I think I begin to see now why people like to own old cars or old wooden boats or original paintings. Of course, some capitalise on this desire and make money out of it but many, unconsciously perhaps, appreciate the latent thought energy that has been poured into the creation. When everybody gathers together to bless a ship, before sliding her into the water, does the outpouring of thought from that gathering form part of that ship and all who sail in her?

But let me return to Eve. She then went on to describe a rather elegant young lady living many years ago in a country house in

Somerset. I was told this person was strongly connected to me, but a few years later I was to grow to know this person very well. At the end of my meeting with Eve she told me that I was on a pathway of spiritual advancement and that I had been meant to make this contact with her to form 'a link in a chain of events'. On this point she either could not or would not elaborate other than to say that it was most necessary for us to have met.

We had got on very well together at that first meeting. I had to admit that I felt drawn towards her and I also felt that she could help me a lot more in my search. But search for what? At that time I did not know except that I seemed to be looking for some kind of truth. I felt, deep inside me, there was something I had to find out. We said our goodbyes and expressed the hope that we would meet again.

One month later I telephoned Eve and asked if she would like to come and visit Brian and me at our home. She eagerly accepted. This meeting at our cottage was to produce the first of many psychic communications that we received through Eve. It was during an evening early in August of 1983 that she first visited us. Apart from giving her our address I had told her absolutely nothing about our home. Within a few minutes of arriving Eve settled and got to work in our small living room.

It may be help to explain, again at this point, that there are many ways in which mediums can 'channel' communication from a discarnate source. They can be totally conscious and aware throughout the process or they can be in a deep trance and totally unconscious of what is going on. Sometimes they can work somewhere between these two conditions, which is to say in a state of high receptivity and yet at the same time in complete control of the proceedings. The type of actual communication can also vary within these various states. It may come through as something the medium 'sees' or 'feels', or as a relayed message in the third person – 'She says that she etc. etc....', or the medium may act as a mouthpiece through which the 'entity' actually speaks, during which the medium's voice or face may undergo considerable change. I am not a practising medium neither do I consider myself, as yet, to be particularly skilled in that direction.

But, when I do undertake channelling work, I find that the most powerful impression that I retain after a session is that of feeling or emotion and it is surprising how much that offers as a clue to the entity who has made contact with me.

I think at this stage I should make it clear that, when talking or writing about psychic matters, it can be very difficult to find the right language. So many of the words have unpleasant connections with lurid ghost stories or with dire warnings from well-meaning 'experts' – who really have little idea what they are talking about. 'Occult', 'spirits', 'entity' are but a few from that list and I can only beg the reader not to be triggered into a negative reaction when I use a word which may not have the right feeling for them. Charity is called for here and an understanding that many such words are used to describe things about which we know very little indeed.

Eve usually works in a relaxed state of awareness and describes what she can see or hear. On this first occasion at the cottage she told us that we were living on a very ancient site, far more ancient than the four hundred years that the cottage had been there. Gradually she began to pick up entities, from the past, connected to the cottage. One of the first of these to make himself known to us was a man who said that he was of a military background and had been the owner of the cottage some years before us. He had bought the cottage for his retirement and had great hopes for it, but died very shortly after arriving. He then went on to say that he enjoyed watching us carry out improvements to the cottage and the garden. He also liked to observe our children growing up as he had had no children of his own. When Brian and I later checked the deeds of the cottage, we found that the first owner, after it had been released from being a tithe cottage in 1945, was a retired army Colonel.

Eve went on to say, apart from the site of the cottage being very ancient, it was also a power site and for that reason it had not only been lived on but also used for psychic orientation in previous times. She told us that she understood Brian and I were the correct people to be in residence now. She then started to move further back in time. A Roman soldier showed himself to Eve, dressed in full uniform, and

we were told that we were living upon some kind of Roman site –
not a residential site but a Roman barracks. The soldier did not live
here, but was on duty guarding the boundary line of a fortress or
garrison. We were then told that we were living on, or very close to
a Roman travelling route and that, in the ground beneath us, there
could be found evidence of this Roman occupation.

As can be imagined, Brian and I were very excited by the quality of communication we were receiving. It was all so interesting and it was taking us into an area of exploration we could never have anticipated. Since we had arrived at the cottage we had been most curious to find out about its history. We knew it was about four hundred years old and that it had been an estate tithe cottage for most of that time. But, we had not given any thought to a time before it was built. Eve, herself, was also fascinated by the information she received and asked if we would consider allowing her to return again to work at a trance level of mediumship. Under those conditions she felt that it would be possible to improve the quality of communication considerably and we would be able to gain a deeper insight into the situation. She asked if she might bring a friend along with her next time who worked as a healer. She had only recently acquired the skill of working at trance level and she felt it advisable to have someone with knowledge and expertise to watch over her whilst she was in trance. We agreed to meet again in two weeks time and parted company greatly encouraged by our experience.

The day after Eve's visit Brian and I set out to find as much as we could about the history of the area around our cottage. We ended up at Poole Museum where we found out that about half a mile from the cottage, there had been a Roman fortress and that excavations had already been carried out there during the building of a bypass. We were already aware that a bridle track, a quarter of a mile away from the cottage and along which we used to walk our dogs and ride our horses, followed the course of an old Roman road.

Many readers will, I expect, feel that Eve may have known about the Roman connection with the area before coming to see us. All I can say is that this was not so and there was, and is, no question of deception. We were not paying Eve for her services. For her to spend her time and money on research, just to impress us, would have been a great waste of effort. I appreciate, though, that the problem of proving no deception is extremely difficult. When any hard facts are given during a communication they can only be proved by going to some form of existing record. As soon as that record is found, it can then be claimed that the medium knew all about it in the first place! Our case is no exception to this problem. On the other hand, the accuracy of the forecasts and the prophecies that we received are much more difficult to ignore, particularly as many of them were taped at the time and deposited with a local bank.

In 1988 a Roman military road was uncovered in the field behind our cottage, just fifty yards from the front door. Eve had told us we were living close to an ancient travelling route. It is unlikely that in August of 1983 she would have had access to that sort of information. She continued to give us more and more evidence that we were able to confirm through research. We were at the beginning of what was going to become a strange tale of reincarnation.

CHAPTER SIX

During one evening in late August, 1983 Eve arrived, to attempt trance communication. With her came her husband, Jim, Cyril, the healer and his wife Audrey. We settled down in the lounge of our cottage, with its heavily beamed ceiling and deep Inglenook fireplace. After chatting for a bit we sat quietly in our armchairs as Eve started to relax sufficiently to move into a trance. We had placed a tape recorder close to her and, from now on, we were going to record every meeting. After some ten to fifteen minutes of peaceful meditation, Eve began to speak, very slowly in a noticeably deeper, more masculine voice. This is what was recorded that evening:

'There is such beauty here, an improvement from past years. The atmosphere is conducive to the work that will be done throughout the coming years. But I am forgetting that I must be a little more considerate to my hosts this evening.

I would greet the both of you and introduce myself. I am known to these that sit here with you as the Reverend Thomas. Our young control is becoming used to my touch and so I would be the first to entrance her, to give her the confidence and the state of peace within that is so necessary for the work that is being attempted. We are most aware of the pull to your heartstrings these last few years. Your patience has been tried as has also your devotion. We make no apologies for these matters for your spirits are quite capable of understanding why this needs to be so.

There was a time when the two of you were most familiar with these lands that are around you. There was a time when all but one of you, that are gathered here, were quite familiar with each other, for you all belonged to the same tribe of people. This may surprise you a little but, it should not, for have you not become aware that all things are planned for a greater purpose than can be proved within one lifetime? I know that you have an appreciation of the arts of re-occurring lives and situations but, I would like you though, to have an understanding why the 'fisher of men' has drawn you together.

There was upon this ground a group of men of great wisdom. Some called them sages; it was a great time ago. I believe we could say within earth years that we are travelling back to a time that is well over 3000BC. In those times the area was sparsely populated. There were what one could term hermits around and they would lead a singular life for a singular purpose. They were greatly skilled in the arts of obtaining and gathering information from the beginning of time and to take it way before into the time to come. It was their duty to place upon this land a covenant, and this was done, and this land and its covenant must always, down through all times, be protected from those who are not of spiritual awakening.

We know that your knowledge goes reasonably deep and that your hearts and minds are pure. You have been well tested, for the responsibility that we would place upon your shoulders will be a heavy burden. There are the necessary tools locked within the bowels of the earth to provide, in more than one direction, and we charge you with the future, for you will be granted some of those treasures that are much admired upon your earth. These treasures are of little interest to we of spirit, though we have a deep respect for the problems of your material world. We know that dues must be met and we are thankful that you have given every last ounce of faith and coinage and trust into this project of the future. Your faith will be well rewarded.

There will be in the next five years, openings that will return in many fold, that which you have freely given. We ask you to hold fast to your faith and to your trust. Do not allow it to be shaken for there is no need. All will, in due course of time, become upon your earth of such an awakening knowledge as to give you much happiness and business. As time goes by others, who are also able to be of use in this enterprise of the future will be drawn to you. Your little shoppe is a sweet beginning but, it is as the bee to the honey. We will show you in three years from now, that which will take you into the dawning of the new age for both of you. Your little shoppe will grow into something that will surprise even you. I thank you kindly for bidding me welcome but, now I know that you will be most pleased to hear another speak with you. I will just stand aside a little but, I will not leave. Those of you that are capable of seeing, will see me standing between the chairs of the one that is the husband and the one that we use, for she is my charge this night.'

It is clear from his remark: *'Our young control is becoming used to my touch'*, that Eve had already had communication from this gentleman before meeting Brian and me. The reader will recall that when I first visited Eve in her flat in Bournemouth, she had said that I was meant to meet her to form a 'link in a chain', although she could elaborate no further at that time and she also had no idea, at that meeting, that I would request to see her again. The only reason she was here this evening was because I had felt inwardly drawn towards her and because I felt she could help me further in my search for answers to questions deep within me. It was now quite apparent to me why my meeting with her had formed the 'link' in a chain of events'.

The Reverend Thomas 'stepped to one side', and a few seconds later we received the voice of a very pompous sounding gentleman coming through the voice box of Eve.

'She is pretty that one. Yes, I approve, I approve. Upon this site they had so many hags at times, ancient crones who were not much to look at. I prefer one such as you, my dear that is pleasing on the eye. The stench here at times – phew! It makes one want to cover one's nostrils. But I would come in upon my horse for I had a house but five miles hence. I would come into this abode for here was one who had a great deal of wisdom and she would help us with love potions and she would give us many potions to help us when we suffered with some awful diseases such as – they are really beyond me. I prefer to allow the women to do the caring and nursing for it is not the place of a place of a gentleman to be seen in the bed-chamber of the sick. This old woman was different although the smells, at times, were a little hard to bear.

She had words of great wisdom that I used to enjoy listening to and, though I know now that is was a sin, she would give me potions that would help with the servants that got with child too often. You know, I am sure, what I am saying to you for it is not for a gentleman to talk too closely of such matters. There were problems, but this old crone would help us in many ways and I would sit around her hearth, most interested in what she would say to me, for though she was thoroughly uneducated and coarse in many ways her wisdom was wide and great. It had its fascinations and, without her aid, life would have been a great deal more complicated for the gentlemen of the countryside.

So we have much to be thankful for and you, pretty young maid, have also got the capabilities of seeing that which is of other worlds, as did the crone, though your knowledge is not as deep as hers. You should work at those parts of you and then you would see more, my dear. You would see others who also lived about here in my time. In those days we had quite a power of control upon the hills and valleys from miles around this cottage. The hamlet was owned by us, by my generation and by others of my family for many generations before me. It passed out of family's control in the sixteenth century and you will find, within your legal documents, a multitude of changes after that.

I have watched your searching and been interested but your documents are far from complete for, in the sixteenth century, many were destroyed for all time. You are the rightful tenants of this property. I would say that to you, and here you must stay. And we will, together, make attempts to put right the wrongs so that your stay may be of a long period and satisfactory to both yourselves and to us, who still watch and guard the true meaning and content of these lands.

The blessings of the Lord God will walk with you and the many who guard and guide your fortunes and shelter you in the storms, but the worst of them is now over for both of you for though, at this moment, it would seem that both of you are greatly ravished by the strength of the storms that have hurtled and blown and stamped around you, take faith in the knowledge that the winds have abated and the sun is beginning to shine through the branches with a greater strength.

We bid you farewell, our little princess, for that, to us, is what you are. Farewell'.

This, presumably landed, gentleman refers to us being *'...greatly ravished by the strength of the storms that have hurtled and blown and stamped around you...'* and the Reverend Thomas says: *'We are thankful that you have given every last ounce of faith and coinage and trust into this project of the future'.*

So we, Brian and I, were here for a purpose! It was something to do with the cottage and the land. It required us to remain here for a while. I can now explain to the reader the relevance of these statements. As you are already aware Brian and I were, prior to this evening, quite sure ourselves about the therapeutic value of the land on which we lived. We had seen the reaction it had upon visitors to my shop. I have also told you of our approaches to the adjoining land owner, approaches to the local authority and about gaining planning permission for a larger floral and general craft venture. All these actions were not only time consuming but also quite expensive to follow through and we were beginning to feel the financial pressure. Brian was finding that his business was not as profitable as it had been. Financial times, in the country as a whole, were difficult around that period of high inflation and recession. Many businesses were going under and we were hanging on by our finger tips.

When Eve withdrew from the trance state she seemed quite tired. Before leaving she gave us the tape recording of the session, telling us to contact her if we wanted to go on with the work. Left to ourselves, we pondered on the extraordinary events of the evening. We felt stunned. We had not given any thought to such a depth of purpose in this life-time and, certainly, we had not considered what we might have done in any previous lives. It is not every day that a person receives such information and it was most difficult to grasp or accept the weight of the responsibility placed upon our shoulders. Indeed we did not accept it. We wanted further proof.

We wanted to share the information with somebody else, if only to find out whether or not they thought it could be a possibility. A few days later we asked some of our closest family to listen and all were wary and concerned. We should be very cautious, they said, in case it was some kind of hoax that spirit entities might be playing on us.

We had asked for advice but we listened to it with only half an ear. Nonetheless in spite of our anxiety we were intrigued, even excited, and having come this far we did not feel like turning back. We felt that we should follow it through if only to prove whether or not we were involved in some fantasy or a different dimension of reality. We already suspected that this was no hoax, for much that had been said had touched on our inner feelings. Somehow, we felt that in coming to the cottage, we had, in some strange way, returned home.

The statements made by the Reverend Thomas and the landed gentleman served to offer us comfort. However, as time passed and my story progresses, it is clear to see that Brian and I put too much emphasis upon the possible financial rewards of our land. We believed that the situation would be taken care of for us. How wrong we were! Our worldly situation was ours to handle to the best of our ability. But we were tackling it without respecting the spiritual guidance that was available and, as a result, we suffered much distress and frustration. We are both much wiser now and, although the experience was painful at the time, we have learned a lot and grown as a result of that pain. In hindsight I can see that the conflicts within me at the time, to do with my cultural and religious upbringing, wielded a powerful negative energy that dissipated my trust in my own intuition.

CHAPTER SEVEN

During the early years of life in our cottage, whilst I was pursuing my psychic interest through books and in circle development work, I always seemed to have, at the back of my mind, an idea that there was something incorrect about my fascination for the subject as a whole. Some kind of guilt feelings kept intruding and eventually, I could see that I would have to choose between institutional religion and the spiritual path now opened up to me. I was, in truth, being offered far more than the dusty old dogmas of the Bible, but traditions die hard and the penalty for changing them is guilt. One medium I met, during that period of my life, picked up with inner turmoil and suggested that I should meet a friend of hers who was an Anglican Vicar at a church in Bournemouth.

I had several meetings with this enlightened man. He was totally tuned into the whole subject of psychic phenomena and, yet somehow managed to fit it into his work as an Anglican Vicar. He understood my predicament perfectly and went to great pains to assure me that I was not offending anybody or anything in my quest. After a full and lengthy discussion he took me into his church and gave me a blessing.

This vicar achieved a great deal for my future spiritual liberation, but not everybody can receive such enlightened treatment from the church. Most people will say that they have not been over-influenced by religious education at school, but, if invited to add up the hours spent at assembly each week, formal lessons of Religious Education, Sunday school and taking into account the religious attitudes of some of the more enthusiastic teachers, the time spent on religious persuasion is very considerable.

I must admit to a certain gratification that our two children, Lisa and Paul, do not seem to suffer from the guilt problems that I used to experience when I was their age. I think it is fair to say that any restrictive religious influence that may have affected them during their time at school, was balanced by our totally open reaction to any strange experiences they may have had. When I ask them if knowledge on the subject of psychic phenomena has been a hindrance or a help, they both assure me that it has enhanced the value of their own lives and helped them cope with the world around them. Both only vaguely remember any religious education that they received at school and I assume from this that, when I was educated, more emphasis was placed upon the subject.

When Eve first came to the cottage the children were at Upper School near Wimborne. Paul was aged fifteen and Lisa seventeen. Up to this time we had not told them about the direction our lives seemed to be taking and though we had answered their questions openly and frankly, they were still ignorant about the way our spiritual lives were developing. I think I felt the need to protect them from the confusion besetting us, as we were barely able to sort out our own questions. To foist our confusions on to the children seemed unfair. However, there comes a time when children reach an age of awareness that cannot be denied and the time had come to start owning up to what we were about.

Religion was not something we had discussed with the children at any great length. We had avoided the subject because of our own uncertainty. We had tried to develop their sense of responsibility and encourage them to respect plants and animals but that, we felt, was about as far as we could go. But now the time of reckoning was upon us and it was going to be difficult.

I was very aware, and so was Brian, that we had a responsibility not to damage our children. This must be the same problem that other parents face when they discover beliefs contrary to the old religious dogmas. I suspect that this is a paradox that will create increasing problems as the Aquarian Age begins to take effect. On the one hand we have the ancient dogma of a religion that demands unquestioning acceptance of some rather strange beliefs and theories. On the other hand, there is an increasing need to develop the individuality of our children so that they become capable of resisting the negative influences of an extremely materialist society. At times we wondered if we were on the correct path but, even if we had been sure, we did not feel that we had the right to cram our beliefs into the children. Their lives belonged to them and the mere fact that they had been born of Brian and me did not mean they had to think as we did. There seems, to me, little point in going through the process of life if you are expected to be a mirror image of your parents. At the same time, it has to be admitted that children look to their parents for guidance. It may be that the best form of guidance parents can give comes from a discreet blend of honesty and concern.

Somehow we managed to get across to Lisa and Paul that we were trying to find out the truth about religion. We said that we felt that when a person died they did not, in fact, 'go' completely. We told them that we knew certain people who had the ability to speak to people who had been dead for some time. Such dead people, we said, could sometimes help people living on earth today. They seemed to accept our explanation without trouble and were neither frightened nor perplexed. Indeed, they accepted the ideas very lightly, as I suppose young people, do, for after all, they were far more interested in the world that they knew rather than the one they did not know. In fact, these days, they readily admit that they used to laugh a little at us and sometimes thought we were a bit strange.

From the age of two, Paul seemed filled with a great energy and zest for life. I had been told his sex plus the date and time of his birth eight months before he arrived and I was also warned that he would be highly psychic in later life. From age five onwards he often said things which seemed far more profound and wise than one might expect at that age. He seemed to carry, within, certain truths and I assume that these must have come from a previous life. He has always had a gregarious personality. His perception of life and people has now become quite astute, as have his visual psychic abilities. Whereas Brian and I usually sense the presence of entities, or beings, or whatever they might be called, Paul will actually see them, often with startling clarity.

He is very aware of his own psychic abilities and has been from an early age. During our years at the cottage he kept seeing a lady on the landing and in his bedroom. He described her as wearing a long black dress with a long white apron tied with a large bow and with crossing straps. She would just appear and observe him. The first time he saw her he said he was startled, but not frightened. She never attempted to communicate with him and neither did he with her. I must say at this point that I was also aware of a similar lady around the children when they were young, especially when they were ill. There came from her a feeling of love and care of children, as though from a nanny or nurse.

As time went by Paul began to see more and more. During the last two years of life at the cottage he saw Roman soldiers on a number of occasions as he worked in the garden. They would just stand around looking at him. He described them as being dressed in red and black skirts, with armour on the top part of the body attached by black leather straps. They had metal helmets with a red vertical band.

One winter evening whilst sitting inside the cottage he became aware of such a Roman pulling on his arm and, visually only, he experienced this Roman taking him out into the garden and onto an area of the driveway where he was joined by more Roman soldiers. They held his arm and made him look into a very deep hole in our driveway. The hole was about twenty five feet deep and twelve feet by fifteen feet wide. At the bottom was a huge piece of stone. I was in the room as Paul experienced this sensation and I could see that he had become very hot and flushed during the experience. He said that although he was aware of being in our driveway which was, at the time, surrounded by trees and bushes, the whole area had appeared, instead, as being very open, without any trees, and he could sense some kind of dry stone wall in the field adjacent to the cottage.

It was about this time that Paul started to experience psychic visions which were unpleasant in that they always involved road accidents. He saw one such accident, which he felt sure would involve Brian, and he asked him not to drive along a certain route for some time. The stretch of road concerned was notorious for accidents and I suspect that Paul was picking up etheric emanations of past accidents on that road and he was interpreting them to concern his own family. This is the type of psychic experiences that Brian's Mother had often been dogged with. I told Paul to make a mental request that such experiences be taken away from him and I also introduced him to a psychic development expert and friend of mine, who agreed also that this was the best course of action for Paul to adopt.

However, from time to time, Paul continued to have similar experiences, particularly when driving late at night, too fast and too tired. We came to the conclusion that these were warnings for him to slow down and served as a form of protection. One of these incidents was taken up by another medium friend of mine, when he saw Paul, and he was able to elaborate a little further on these experiences. Paul had been driving home one night, very late, and felt a great pain in his head, chest, arms and legs which took several hours to go away. Again it appeared to be emanations from a road accident. My friend was able to tell Paul that it was, in fact, a friend of Paul's, who had died in a road accident twelve months before. He was trying to warn, not Paul, but another friend who knew Paul, to take much greater care when driving. The name of the boy at risk was given and the information duly passed on to him by Paul.

The visions eventually seemed to have left Paul, but, one evening, he described to me seeing what he said was the nearest thing to a fairy he had ever witnessed. I knew from his description that he had seen a nature spirit, part of the Deva or Nature Kingdom. It was an area of psychic phenomena about which he had absolutely no knowledge but I knew it to be a good and pure level of communication and I was pleased that he appeared to be graduating to higher realms of contact. The vision he experienced was of a small, impish-like gnome with a mischievous smile on its face. An absolutely typical garden gnome except that this was not made of plastic but appeared from a hedge and then disappeared. I urge the reader not to be too eager to scoff. What Paul was seeing was some form of spirit emanation that was connected with plants and trees. It was necessary for him to sense it in some visible form, so why not a gnome? For that is the traditional form for our garden earth spirits. When we buy a plastic gnome from the nearest garden centre and plant him, legs astride, arms akimbo, beside our pond, are we not recognizing and personifying, quite unconsciously, the nature life of our garden? Why else would we put the little man there?

Having read all this, my reader might well imagine Paul to have been some kind of angelic youth. Not at all, he was full of life and energy and into everything one might expect a young lad of his age would be – cars, music, girls, holidays and general fun. I think it is terribly important to stress how vital it was that this should be so.

His psychic powers could not be denied and, because they were so powerful, it was essential that they should be balanced by a healthy enjoyment of this physical life. Perhaps, later in life, he would wish to explore the other dimensions open to him and, indeed, use them for the good of others. But, I think at the time, his task was to come to terms with the physical world and the best way to do that was for him to enjoy it. Even so, he recognized the potential within himself and was starting to apply it. Other young people seemed to be attracted to him. They respected his psychic experiences, about which he is very frank and open, and they accepted his advice and counsel if they were troubled.

Lisa had a very different character from Paul. She did not show any signs, at that stage, of outward psychic abilities. What she did manifest was an ability to read people. I was told, at one stage, that Lisa, like Paul, would make good use of her psychic abilities at a later time in her life.

She was a talented child, academically, musically, artistically and athletically. She could have developed any one of these talents but chose to work with her artistic ability, against the advice of her teachers, who would have preferred to see her pursue an academic career. From a very early age I sensed that Lisa found outsiders difficult to get on with, so I was particularly interested when William Thomas stated, in one of his sessions, that Lisa had not lived an Earth life for a very considerable time. She had chosen to return, in this life, as my daughter, a relationship that we had shared in a previous lifetime. Because of the long time she had spent in another dimension she was finding it difficult to adjust to the Earth way-of-life. She found it particularly difficult to come to terms with the insincerity of others. Though I have no statistics to prove it, I suspect that most children who have strong psychic awareness, have this powerful inbuilt sense of justice and concern. I would hasten to add that this does not necessarily mean that they are angels!

There is an understanding, among enlightened people today, that many souls are returning to Earth for the particular purpose of using their deep inner knowledge to assist their fellow beings through the transition into the Aquarian Age. One cannot but feel concern for such souls, launched into a materialistic culture, for the guardians of our religious welfare seem to show little understanding for their problems. Theology and spirituality make uneasy bedfellows.

Lisa turned to her artistic abilities for a career and became a natural history illustrator. Paul turned to farming and, as he had a natural ability to work with machinery, he concentrated on mechanised farming and machinery in general.

Family life is never easy. It consists of a mix of personalities, all trying to get on together under one roof. In many respects we were no different from any other family. Yet we were different in that Brian and I were upon a path of self-exploration which seemed to be guided, and, yet, was very confusing and unsettling. We had the normal family problems of children growing up and trying to find themselves within the confines of family life. We also had the considerable responsibility of being self-sufficient and self-employed which, of necessity, limits free time. When you work for yourself you never ever leave it behind. Our life has been one of extreme hard work, both physically and mentally. Luckily Brian and I had a driving force and intuition within, which we gradually learned to harness and apply. Everybody has this inner guidance and I believe many problems could be answered if it is used. Hopefully this story of ours will encourage others to look for hidden abilities within themselves, because using such gifts will gradually improve the quality of their own lives and those with whom they come into contact.

We had one great advantage that enabled us to survive many pressures. We seemed always to be in total harmony with one another. We understand, from the psychic information that we have received from various sources, that we are not strangers to each other in this lifetime and our union this time was presumably planned by us. Without the strength of this age-old union I could not have continued to pursue my search for truth and can only assume I would not have reached the point I am at today.

CHAPTER EIGHT

Before I go on with the main story there is an apparently superficial, but interesting, event I must recall here which happened one summer evening, around the time that I first met Eve. Brian and Paul and one of the sheepdogs were in the garden at dusk, approximately 9 p.m. Suddenly, and most vividly, appearing before them all was a pure white goat. What was so startling was its position, about one foot above ground level, and the silence with which it passed across the garden, through the hedge and into the next field, not disturbing the hedge in any way as it did so.

Had Brian and my son been the only ones to see this 'ghostly goat' I may not have believed them when they told me. However, what served to convince me that they had not imagined it was the reaction of our sheepdog. He had been most alarmed and fearful of what he could see. He sank down on his haunches and lay low until the goat disappeared. His normal reaction to another animal in his garden, be it fox, dog, cat or human stranger, would have been to rush at it and bark. What he saw was obviously unusual to him and he was ill at ease with the experience. He was more than glad to get inside the cottage as soon as possible.

We thought no more of the event other than to tease one another about going into the garden at dusk and running the risk of seeing the 'ghostly goat'. I would say that it was not something that worried us unduly and it somehow added a special touch to the ancient cottage and its garden.

However, about six months later I went to visit an old lifelong friend in London for a few days. During one of our conversations, knowing my interest in psychic matters, my friend related a piece of information given to her by an acquaintance who happened to be a medium. This lady had described the friendship between the two of us since childhood and went on to say that she knew I lived in an old thatched cottage in Dorset and further that I kept a beautiful, pure white goat in my garden. My friend, knowing this not to be so, remarked that I had two sheepdogs, some cats, rabbits, guinea pigs and horses but no goat. She would, however, check this point when she next saw me. As you can imagine, she was more than taken aback when I related the tale of the 'ghostly goat'.

It is a blessing in life, if we allow it to be so, that we can look back after only a short time and view a period of trial and tribulation with a certain detachment, even humour. And so, when Brian and I look back on the days when our relationship with William Thomas was developing, we recall a rich mix of anxiety, physical exhaustion and lively family activity. We always took time off at the weekends to walk the Dorset countryside and the cheerful unconcern of the children and our tribe of animals did much to remove the burdens from our shoulders. We had a caravan for a few years in which we used to explore places further afield. On one such exploration in North Wales we came across a stone circle marked by a ring of quite small stones. We became quite excited at our find and I remember insisting that the four of us should hold hands and dance around the circle. I knew next to nothing about stone circles and yet I instinctively sensed the spiritual power or energy that was contained within those stones. We will find ourselves in much closer relationship with stone circles later in my story.

One continuing task that took our energy was the renovation of the cottage. This physical labour, though arduous and expensive, did much to keep our minds in healthy balance between the realities of the physical and spiritual dimensions. The cottage was a typical old country cottage, built of cob with a thatched roof and with no foundations whatsoever. It literally sat on the earth!

Brian and I and the children put a great deal of ourselves into that cottage and there were many incidents that make us all laugh when we look back on those times. One day we decided to remove the old fireplace in the living room, hoping to discover an old Inglenook. No Egyptian tomb was opened with greater care, or more heightened excitement than that aged fireplace. The tension rose as Brian prepared to knock away the last few bricks. Suddenly a deep rumbling sound was heard and the room was filled with half a ton of rubble and soot, avalanching down from the chimney breast in which it had been pent up maybe a century ago. We just stood there, all four of us, peering blackly at each other through the layers of soot and dust that covered everything. The animals had deserted us, with singular alacrity, and were cowering in some remote corner of the garden. But, emerging through the swirling clouds stood our Inglenook! We had no hot water at that time as the plumbing was also being re-instated, but, at the end of the day, we managed to clean ourselves up by boiling pots and kettles of water. The dogs, to their great delight, were taken down to the sea for a bathe.

Another of our projects was to build an extension on to one side of the cottage. This required the usual footings but the cottage was sitting on top of several springs, which play no small part in the later chapters of this story. Every morning, when we went outside we found the footings would be full of water. All four of us would have to get bailing away to keep the level of the water down. On one such morning we were most anxious to clear the water completely as we were expecting a visit from the local authority building inspector. During the course of bailing out, Brian dislocated his back and we had to drag him on to the kitchen floor. He remained there for some considerable time, including the duration of the building inspector's visit. We laugh when we look back at the bizarre situation of the inspector discussing building technicalities with Brian who was prostrate upon the floor. The gentleman showed no sign of emotion, whatsoever, about holding a conversation with a person in such a state, but the children and I were giggling hysterically in the adjoining room.

At one stage we installed a large log-burning boiler to heat the cottage and water system. On the day of installation the system developed a terrible airlock – the explosions and crashing from the boiler and its pipes were beyond belief. The children and I were terrified and fled into the garden to join the animals in their now accustomed refuge. For many weeks I wrestled with that boiler, trying to control it, before the system finally settled down.

We were always most vigilant, when knocking down walls in the cottage, to search for items buried deep with the cob, but all we ever found were a few pony shoes placed there for good luck by the builder of the cottage. Because of this, when we filled in areas of wall, we placed items into it for somebody to find in the future and, in Paul's bedroom, we put a plastic box in the wall full of items relating to the age that we live in. We also left a written note saying that the finder was a lot luckier than we had been in uncovering hidden treasures!

During the winter months, following our first trance communications from the Reverend Thomas, Brian and I came up with the idea that it might be possible to open our garden to the public during the summer months, by joining a national gardens organisation which passed proceeds from such openings to charity. We made an application to the organisation – the garden was inspected for suitability and was immediately accepted.

Our first opening was on a Sunday afternoon in June of 1985. We were amazed and delighted at the response. We had three hundred and fifty visitors to that garden in just one afternoon. We opened the garden on summer Sundays for several years to follow, always with a very high turn-out of visitors. Many people returned month after month and year after year. Many, many times people told us about the effect the garden and cottage had on them. Often they returned, with friends, to witness the experience. All commented on the peace and the feeling that they had stepped into another world just by coming up our winding driveway.

Brian and I were very keen to trace the Reverend WilliamThomas and to find out who he was, what place and period of time he came from. From the statements made by the landed gentleman, who spoke following the Reverend Thomas on that first evening, we felt it likely that they both hailed from Dorset, probably within the last four hundred years of our cottage's existence.

We went to Dorchester to trace the church records of Dorset. We found that a Reverend William Thomas had been the rector at a small village near Wimborne from 1576 to 1619. It seemed most likely that this was our communicator as we could trace no other clergyman with the name of Thomas in Dorset in the period of our cottage. We also discovered some further information about William Thomas from the records which we noted, but decided to keep very much to ourselves, in the hope that he would confirm certain points in later communications. We discovered that he had been involved in a court case against the Lord of the Manor of Long Crichel, of which he was Rector in 1579. This was over a disagreement about tithe apportionments. We also discovered that in the seventeen hundreds, when William Thomas was no longer alive, the parsonage in which he had once lived had been submerged in a large man-made lake, together with the original village.

What was so uncanny for us, when we discovered the possible location of William Thomas, was the fact that for several years prior we had been drawn to walking the footpath on the Crichel Estate on numerous occasions. Out of all the locations we could have chosen to walk in Dorset, we felt continually drawn to Crichel!

Once we felt that we had confirmed the Reverend Thomas's existence we were more than keen to receive further communication from him, so as to gain more information to work on. We used the method of trance communication through Eve several times during the following three years. Gradually we obtained a fuller picture of my relationship with this deceased parson and the reasons for re-kindling it. Tape recordings were kept of all communications received and I will now give some excerpts of material received soon after we had first traced a William Thomas in the county records:-

'It is most pleasant to speak with you once again, to share the pleasure of your small abode. Yes the light within is like the light of a very large Christmas tree. The vision from your hearthside can be seen quite a long way, my children. Steadily we have seen it burn brighter and brighter as the years have flowed. Earlier this evening I heard a conversation about time. I have been aware of each one of you for several years, probably more years than it would be wise to tell you. In the earliest days each one of you resided in different parts

of the country. Slowly you have been brought together for a purpose. A purpose planned and decided amongst you before your lifetime upon earth. Take comfort and strength, in the future years, from the knowledge that you have known each other for much longer than your few earth years.'

I must make mention here that this phenomenon of people coming together, or being brought together for a purpose, seems to be more accepted these days. Dr. Arthur Guirdham brought emphasis to it some thirty years ago with his work on Cathar reincarnations. His work produced evidence of group reincarnations.

'You are working quite well now following the clues with a great deal of expertise. Then that is to be expected when you have myself guiding you and putting into your minds those thoughts of curiosity that encourage you to leave your work and go and seek. Though the seeking has been hard, it has also been quite exciting has it not madame?

I was never a man to hide myself. I have two firm feet that I stand upon. That was always my way. There was no need for me to hide from those men of little understanding in my time or from the annals of time itself. For I hold the key to a puzzle that was originally more than a small part of my creation. There is still another book for you to find. It is a large heavy book that would be difficult for you to pick up. You will find further information of my legal dealings with the Squire.

I understand why you like to find your proofs. I appreciate the honesty of the reasoning and so it is my promise to encourage you in your seeking. Around the time of the full moon, within the month of March, so you will find a build-up within your own minds, your instincts will grow stronger my dear. Trust them, for you have been led carefully from month to month and your own capabilities of sensing and seeing have improved. Give yourselves a little longer to delve in your books. Be most careful that, in writing, you put down each date correctly, for there will be many who will search the records and try most hard to bring them to discredit, but stand firm, you have your records, they are the real proof.

There is another one who is needed to guide and help you in those records. He is a gentleman now reaching the age of wisdom, getting a little frail, but with a mind that is sharp and alive and used to searching amongst old manuscripts. Work closely with him. He has those special skills that you require to make doubly sure that your facts are true.

Have you seen the ducks that play among the spires of my small house of God? This is one of the delights of my newer body. I can now walk where I please and none of the elements of Earth can stay me. You understand?'

It is clear that William Thomas is enjoying and approving of the fact that we are attempting to trace and prove the validity of his existence and his communication. In fact, he even directs us in certain areas. He has now confirmed that he had legal dealings with the Squire and he mentions that ducks now swim about the roof of his once 'small house of God'. We have to assume that we have now found out who William Thomas was and is. It was also at this stage that William Thomas started to indicate the need to develop my own psychic abilities in order to understand and find the 'treasures of the site'. When he talks about 'spirit', I assume he refers what we call 'soul'. This aspect of our being is receiving much more emphasis as we approach the Aquarian Age. He says:

'Have faith. Remember that those powers do not just belong to you, the young lady who lives on Earth at the moment. They are loaned to you from the greater powers and it is your spirit who is the true custodian. So there is no need for you to have a lack of faith, for it is not you that is the custodian, but your spirit. It is only for you to learn to work with your spirit. That is simple, it is not? It is most natural. I will walk with you and teach you further, for it is my delight. I spend a lot of time with you on this property that makes me feel at peace, for I missed not owning such a property those many

years ago. The right of owning was snatched from my hands, and my spirit cannot rest until one or two wrongs are put right. But that is my story and not yours and it is God's story to take from this land that which is his, for the work that is of his choosing. We know that you are deeply respectful of this truth and that is why such a responsibility was placed with you both, a few years ago, when your children were children.'

His concern for material values is interesting; the wrongs of four hundred years ago (using linear time) have still to be corrected. But as my psychic skills develop, it will be seen that William Thomas's perception of his own situation also develops, and he becomes less and less concerned with the mundane earthly matters of the past.

He goes on to indicate that I have within me the ability to dowse for artefacts beneath the ground and I have to admit here that, although I realised I could develop this talent, I did not make the effort that I should to master it. I kept looking to others to do this sort of work for me. I must also confess, at that stage, I still exercised a degree of scepticism and found it all very difficult to believe and accept. I was not totally convinced and was wary of just how deeply involved I was prepared to be. I felt, in a way, very much on my own and I wanted to protect myself, my sanity and my family from possible disillusionment. I had to learn to have confidence in myself and, as the reader will find out, I learned the hard way.

William Thomas had indicated that he had been around us for a long time and I could still recall the feeling of being watched over by a Clerical figure in early childhood. In hindsight it is all too clear now for me to see that I was ill-prepared culturally and religiously for what was unfolding in my life and subsequently this caused me to have a lack of trust in my own intuition and discomfort in my thought processes over the coming years. Old habits and patterns die hard!

CHAPTER NINE

William Thomas had told us in his most recent communication:

'There is another one who is needed to guide and help you with those records.'

I did indeed meet such a person who totally fitted the description. It is this person who has spent much time searching the historic records in order that I can give some substance to this story. In a later communication William Thomas tells us that there is a very special area of information, relating to our land, the details of which will not become known to us until a particular man makes contact. In his own words he says:

'We know that you would wish to unlock time but the area that you would unlock has a special seal. There is only one who is capable of breaking that seal. The day that he comes here you will find the deeper evidence. We have only been permitted to part with some knowledge of these facts.'

As predicted, that help arrived in due course but not until we had endured two years of total confusion and had virtually given up all hope of solving the mystery of the land on which we lived.

It was at this time, in the autumn of 1987, that building and road developments were beginning to appear around the cottage. We had become aware of a cloud on our horizon some six months before and we had received a warning about it from William Thomas. Here is what he had to say:

'The boundary line of the property today is considerably altered from the original habitation. In some respects it should curve out-wards into a wider arc. Are you aware of this? I am going back to

*the original boundaries. Before another moon has come and gone, a
part of the land will have come under the hammer of the auctioneers.
In my day it was quite a simple procedure to sell a parcel of land but,
those who sit in judgement in your time are most confusing fellows.
They make most simple things most complicated.'*

We now understood that there had been a change of ownership in
the land alongside our cottage. The original owner had sold to a
building company who had assumed that they would get building
consent. However, a far more alarming situation had also arisen. A
local Draft Development Plan had been published for the comments
of local residents. Imagine our horror to find that in this Draft Plan
our cottage was completely missing and a new housing estate was in
its place.

Brian and I were frantic in our written objections to this future
proposal. How could the local planners even consider demolishing
such a beautiful old cottage with its well matured gardens, to replace
it with a modern housing estate? But we had a lot to learn! There are
many, many people in our society for whom the only purpose in life
is to make money. Making money, as such, is not a bad thing. Indeed,
it is very necessary and can do a lot of good. But, when the process
is divorced from any spiritual ground base it too easily becomes an
obscenity.

In reply to our objections we were told that, because we lived
upon the fringe of the new housing development, we had the choice
to be included in it if we so desired. Many here may say – why did
we not cash in on the situation and take the opportunity to move on?
Apart from our psychic knowledge about the cottage and its land we
had now spent many years renovating it. We had a beautiful garden,
which was open to the public on a regular basis, and I was now
running my own small cottage industry. It did not suit our worldly
situation, let alone the spiritual one, to sell off to a characterless
housing development.

We made it clear to the Local Authority that we did not want to
surrender our cottage and I approached the Listing Authority in an

attempt to have the cottage listed in order to protect its future. Sadly this could not be done as the authority did not consider the property suitable for listing. There had been, they said, too many alterations and additions done to it over the years.

As well as making known our intention to stay, we had to raise the question of an ancient public footpath that ran along the driveway of our cottage before leading into an adjoining field. While the cottage remained in a rural setting we were quite happy that the footpath should run along our drive, but it would become too much of a burden with houses all around us and many more people using it.

We were assured at this stage that, in the event of future housing development, the footpath would be diverted away from the drive. This footpath was to become a major factor in the eventual fate of our cottage. It was the factor that had been foretold long before. A very elderly psychic friend of ours, who was not even aware of the existence of a public right of way, told us that the footpath belonging to the cottage would one day be the 'key to the property'. At the time we had no idea what this was about but, we never forgot it and one day its meaning became only too clear.

The reader will recall that we had been told of 'treasure' buried at the cottage. This news had triggered off an energetic search which lasted for almost two years. Many members of the family were dragged into weekends of endless digging of enormous holes which produced absolutely nothing. When we look back, having since worked alongside experienced archaeologists, our methods were so obviously crude and inefficient. We certainly found no buried hoard and, from the few artefacts we subsequently found close to the surface, it would seem very likely that, if there had been anything there, we would have missed it in our ignorance and clumsiness.

Anyway, though defeated, we were only a trifle deflated. I decided to approach the British Dowsing Society to seek an archaeological dowser. Looking back now, I realise I should not have been looking to others for help in this direction. But, as I have already stated, I had very little belief in my own psychic abilities at that time.

The British Society of Dowsers put us in touch with a highly respected dowser from their organisation. I wrote to him to ask if he would be interested in dowsing on our land for possible archaeological artefacts. I gave him absolutely no information about our psychic adventures and so far as he was concerned, our reason for asking was because the cottage was very ancient. The dowser agreed to come and asked for a map or plan of the cottage and its land so that he could map dowse in his own home first. This was duly sent.

Imagine our excitement when we received a letter from him to say that he was amazed at what he had picked up from his map dowsing. He said it looked as if we had the proceeds of several robberies buried at various points throughout our garden. He added that the buried contents included gem stones, church ornaments, gold and silver. We were beside ourselves with wild excitement. I can only laugh when I look back at the state we got ourselves into. Having read the contents of his letter I was in considerable need of a glass of brandy to calm my emotions. The dowser asked to be allowed to come to the cottage in order to carry out actual site dowsing in order to pin point the areas for us to excavate. Of course we agreed, only too willingly, and a date was set.

During his time spent at our cottage a considerable part of it was taken up with site dowsing and staking out areas for later investigation. I must emphasise that he was a highly respected member of the Society of Dowsers. He was a well-known author of several books on the subject and had achieved many important and valuable finds as a result of his expertise in dowsing. He had an excellent reputation for sensitive and accurate dowsing. At the end of the afternoon, having had a meal with us, he departed leaving us to start excavating the following day. We spent hours painstakingly digging, but again we found absolutely nothing. What was going on – surely despite our primitive methods of searching, something should have turned up?

We made contact to discuss the situation with the dowser. Not only was he most surprised at our failure to uncover anything but he was, as can well be imaged, highly embarrassed. He said that it was possible that the dowsing readings might have been cases of 'remanence'. This means that the objects had been in the ground at one time, but had now been removed, leaving behind energetic indications of their presence capable of being picked up through dowsing. However, he said he had already tested for this phenomenon and did not feel it was the case. He also said that, as we had a considerable amount of clay within our garden, it was possible that the dowsing readings had become confused. Apparently this can sometimes happen when clay is present. At the time of writing nothing of any great moment has been found and we have assumed that, somewhere along the line, a mistake has been made. Nevertheless I still feel that there is something remarkable lying beneath that land which will one day be unearthed.

Brian and I had hoped that the finding of buried treasure would finance the development of a craft project within the garden. You will recall that we had planning permission to enlarge my cottage industry but lacked the finance to do so. We also hoped it would serve to rescue us from our, now, ever-worsening financial situation. By now, I was seriously beginning to question the wisdom of dabbling in psychic matters. I was concerned that I had, maybe, given the children false ideas about a spiritual existence and eternal life. I went through a phase when I absolutely shut out any psychic influences I may have felt and I studied as many religious teachings I could to see if, in any way, I was transgressing some sort of doctrine, or moral code. This was the price I had to pay for the continuing conflict between my inner knowing and my confusing cultural and religious upbringing.

CHAPTER TEN

Our failure to uncover any treasure came as a shock. We had placed far too much faith in our expectation and had tailored our finances accordingly. Recession biting into the economy caused Brian's landscaping business to take a huge drop in turnover. Our life-style would have to be radically changed and so we put the cottage up for sale. Not only were we distraught but also disillusioned and disillusionment was the one thing I had always feared. It was that fear that was behind my reluctance to develop my own psychic abilities. In short, I had no real belief in myself at that time.

Brian and I had made the decision to sell the cottage and move elsewhere, hopefully further into the country, to get away from the housing development starting to eat into the area of Dorset in which we lived. We had also decided to have nothing more to do with psychic matters. We would henceforth live a complete worldly life. We were looking to blame external happenings for our internal failings at that time. Making these brave decisions was one thing, sticking to them was another, for there were powerful influences at work that were not going to let us go that easily.

The cottage went on the market in January 1985 and, in the course of the following eight months, I showed sixty prospective buyers around it. All fell in love with the cottage and its garden and yet we received only one offer of purchase and that was too low for us to be able to even consider it. However, as always, we had yet another very successful season of garden openings with record attendances!

By August of that year we were beginning to get more than a little concerned at our failure to obtain a purchaser for the cottage. We had been out and about looking for a possible new home and had found one or two that we felt we could move to. Eve, knowing of our frustration, suggested we join with her for further communication with the Reverend William Thomas. We agreed, however, with great reluctance. Our attitude towards William Thomas that evening was hostile and frosty. We felt let down by him and wanted to put the blame for our failure at his feet, not ours. As he began to speak I felt he was making excuses. I was not prepared that evening, to absorb his words or even to attempt to accept his comments on our situation. The atmosphere was heavy and William Thomas was well aware of it. Towards the end of the communication I made the statement: 'We will move'. And that was our intention at the end of the evening.

I will now give a verbatim report of that evening's communication but I must first say that its contents meant very little to me on that August evening. However, within one month, following a very strange and moving experience, the communication of that evening was to become a total revelation to me and ultimately the cause of my change of direction. In short, that evening's communication was the most important of any I had received so far. The parson knew me, through and through – how could I continue to doubt and reject him?

'It was a great time ago and before the Romans came and desecrated this precious land and before the Saxons wrecked its peace that it was used for a purpose far more divine. It is from this source that you gain these powers. They go back long before your records though. It is of little use to search records this time though, my dear you did exceedingly well last time. Some areas are still hidden but they are of little interest. You received the most important information, that I am a person in reality, not a figment of imagination. To know that is a comfort to me, working as I do, for I can send forth information of a different calibre to that which I am used to. I know I can work in a more direct manner but, I am more skilled in manipulation. It is most interesting, at times, to watch my words flow beneath a pen and to watch the mind working away believing that the words it was forming were its own.

We know of your continued struggles and of the way you champ at the bit continuously. It has been most frustrating for both of you and I know that there have been many tears shed and many times when your minds and hearts were filled with fear, which has not entirely left you. But from that fear is arising, slowly, a greater *strength and understanding such as you have never had before. It is a cruel lesson and often our hearts cry with you but we must not interfere. There are little things that we can do but we have not the right to change the natural order or to stop you treading the paths that you have chosen to tread.*

The charge that you received many years ago still sits upon your shoulders. You especially, madame, have not entirely released it; though you have made strong attempts to market your home, deep within you is still a strong hold to the underlying responsibilities of the property. I would say to you that each of the children of earth have two minds and, unless both minds work in complete unison, the natural laws of earth will not be obeyed, for the one mind is pulling against the other. Do you understand?'

Me: 'No, not completely.'

William Thomas: *'You know that when thoughts are sent forth, they contain within their construction a certain strength and a power of creation. Not all of them will stay with life in them forever, but some will, and the thoughts that are there, deep within the sub-conscious mind have a greater strength and power than the thoughts of the surface mind.*

If the thoughts of your surface mind, which are closely linked to your problems of earth, do not ride easily with those of your sub-conscious mind and the passage of the soul, then what you create will be torn in two directions. Often I watch you walking in your garden and searching your heart and your mind for the reason why certain things must be. It is then that I try to draw closer to you to encourage your mind to flow along patterns of understanding. But for quite a long time the shadows have been too strong and I have not been able to gain a close enough entry.

We know that one half of your being longs to obey the laws of your land. We know that orders must be met. I had the same problems when I lived on earth. But still I say to you child, you must want your changes with the strength of two minds before the pattern can change along the ways that you would choose.

You have been puzzled, have you not, as to why no purchasers with their bags of gold have walked towards you? Yes, it is confusing to seek the right explanation. But I say to you, with my hand on my heart, and the other on the Holy Book, that is none of our doing. It lies more within your own hearts and minds and thoughts that have brought these laws into being. I would ask you now for your own goodness and the peace within your own mind, to be truly honest and admit that when you have sought other properties and decided that, yes, you would like to have owned them, has there not been, deep within you, one or two tears when you have come back to the arms of this property? But maybe you can understand how your own tears and your own deeper longings have brought into being laws that are not created by your government, but by the powers of much greater strength and being. In your time you call them metaphysical states of being. Does that sound reasonable to you? But you are puzzled, I can see in your mind child.'

Me: 'I am confused.'

William Thomas: *'That is a healthy sign for you to be confused. It means that now you are beginning to look at the situation from more angles than one. It is a good beginning. If you would truly release yourselves from the responsibilities of this property, you are free to do so and you will have our blessing and our help to enable your business affairs to flow correctly. But first you must once again walk in your garden and face the truth that lies deep within you. Converse with your husband and make final conclusions and give your answer to your Creator together in the privacy of your own bedchamber. That is the world that belongs to the two of you.*

You hoped to hear differently I know. I can see it in your mind. But how can we give to you information that is possibly acceptable to you at this moment, but not totally truthful? What is it you do not understand?

You have both been living two lives. The one half of you has been closely involved with the normal responsibilities that a family and the laws of earth bring to you. Only you can truly answer as to whether the both of you have handled your business affairs wisely throughout the past years. We can help in many ways but we can never live your lives for you. We can uplift and can bring the rays that will make you happier and stronger. We can fill your minds when they are pure with the thoughts that will open doorways to other states of being but only if you give us the correct recipe.

The other part of your life has worked a certain way and for quite some time it has stood still and that was not because we made you stand still. That came from yourselves, from your own inner selves, who were trying to manipulate and find answers in wrong directions. So your own spirits, your own subconscious created the blocks which to both of you appeared so frustrating. I do not say pleasing words to you but, words of truth which will take you both forward into a future that is once again expansive. One or two decisions have been made which are healthier than the ones you made earlier in the year. Am I correct? Recently you have altered your minds in one or two ways from those opinions you had at the beginning of this year. You have changed your decisions, not ones concerning the property, but personal decisions which have been most beneficial to your peace of mind.

Have you not noticed that recently, although your problems are still heavy, there is now a freedom, a shaft of light that is bringing into your minds an awareness of other ways in which you could draw to yourselves the answer to some, if not all, of your financial problems?'

This was so, as we had already taken steps to re-mortgage the cottage.

'Do you not agree, or is confusion still there?'
Me: 'I am still confused.'
William Thomas: *'Tell me of that confusion.'*
Me: 'You gave us information two or three years ago of things to be that have not come true.'
William Thomas: *'You are speaking largely of the trinkets that lie hidden in the soil of this property. They still lie hidden. They are here but is was not for you to find them, was it? Otherwise you would have*

found them. They are here. They have been here many centuries and they lie quite deep within the soil. It will take some highly experienced people a long time to find them and the main problems for people such as you, seeking treasures such as these, is that you have very little practice. We know that it is most difficult to have dangerous holes on your property. But still I say that the trinkets are here. We have not told untruths. But they will take a long time to find and experienced hands should organise such a search.

It is a very painstaking task to find tiny objects in a pile of ancient mud. In some of the places the holes would have to go down deeper than you are skilled enough to handle. The natural skills that the daily employment that your husband has gained over the years will give to him the understanding that this piece of land is very different to how it looked two and three thousand years ago. Over the centuries it has developed a depth that is now a good amount higher than in those days when treasures were buried for safety here. The treasures did not belong to the churches of your time. They were treasures that went back before the Christian churches came into being in this part of the country. We are talking of considerable changes in the measurement of the land as it is today. 'Does that take away a little of your confusion?'

Me: 'Yes.'

William Thomas: *'That is good, but your courage is sometimes a little low. Make your choice, the two of you, as to whether you can truly leave this child who has become part of your life, for that is what this property has become. Deep within you, not a house and garden, but a part of your very being and it is to that you must answer.*

Make the decision once and for all and you will find that the waters will once again start to run freely. Instead of me taking from your shoulder the load that has been so hard to carry, it seems that I have placed it even more heavily upon you. But that is not so; we have given to you a little bit of magic that will work that the two of you alone can use the key that will bring life to this magic.

Do you understand or are you still confused?'

Me: 'We will move.'

William Thomas: *'The decision is made on the surface; now make it deep within your being. From this moment on, if it is your choice to leave the property, then you must truly say farewell, and not fret over what will happen when it loses your protection. It will no longer be your responsibility. Have I made myself clear?*

This night, I would that I was capable of joining with you in a glass of claret to lift your spirits. A glass of wine was most beneficial to me when I came home tired and weary from the many problems that were brought to me. I cannot give you a tray with wine upon it but I would ask you please to imagine, that the offering I give you in deep sincerity is as real as the glass of wine I was able to enjoy many years ago, when I walked these hills and vales.

I will withdraw from you now, feeling a little sad, for I know that your hearts are heavy. You hoped to hear something different but, I ask you once again to realize that although we love you dearly, we can only do so much for you. We cannot take away that which you have created, whether it be a creation within your daily lives or a creation through the powers of your spirit. Think kindly of those who work so hard to steer you along the road to enlightenment and the day will come when you will awake and realise that, from this period of trouble and anguish, you have drawn jewels of much greater worth than those that lay in the soil beneath your feet. I leave you the blessings of the God Almighty. Farewell.'

For the rest of that month of August we continued in our attempt to sell our cottage. As I said before, we had not given any great thought to the most recent communication from Reverend William Thomas. We did not like what we had been told that evening perhaps because it was too close to the truth for our own comfort and, at that time, we were not prepared to admit to our mistakes. Looking back, it is not difficult for us to see now that, apart from our financial situation forcing the sale of our cottage, we were almost trying to sell as a gesture of protest – an expression of our disappointment at the way things had turned out. As I have said before, we looked to place the blame for our failings at the feet of the Reverend Thomas.

An event during the early part of the following month of September served to force first me and then Brian, to look deeper into ourselves for our motives and our true inner feelings about that cottage and its land.

I had gone into the field next to the cottage, one afternoon, to feed our three horses some hay. I was making a fuss of them as they munched away steadily when, suddenly, from two fields away there was an eruption of noise from a huge earth excavating machine. I had not seen it there as I went to feed the horses and suddenly it had burst into action.

My reaction shocks me even to this day when I think about it. I fell on the ground sobbing. I felt as if my heart was being torn out. I banged my fists on the ground screaming 'No! No!' In the middle of this outbreak of torment I could sense William Thomas saying to me:

'Go inside the cottage and listen to the recording of what I had to say to you one month ago. Perhaps then you will understand why you feel this extreme pain and emotion as you witness the machine tearing at the ground.'

I flew inside and found the tape recorder. As I listened to William Thomas's words, this time with an open mind, I could only too clearly see that they contained extraordinary wisdom. One part of me, the surface worldly me, was trying to sell and move. Yet, deep within, that was not my desire and the two parts of me were in conflict – causing confusion and anger and sorrow. Deep within me this land meant more than I could understand at that time and when I saw it being violated, something deep within me stirred. Somehow, I had to find out why I felt this pain and why this land meant so much to me.

When Brian came home that evening we had a deep discussion regarding these events and he, once again, listened to William Thomas's communication of the previous month. The result was that we decided we just could not leave the land although, why, we still did not understand. We had to obey our inner feelings because they were too potent to disregard.

This message was a turning point in my life. I now began to understand the complexity and the great power of thought. It is a power that gives us the ability to direct our lives. At last the light was beginning to shine in the dark castle of my soul. I could see that there was the possibility of joy ahead for me if I could but continue to listen to myself. Of course we still had a critical financial position. Nevertheless we decided to take the cottage off the market for the time being and to make every effort to improve our financial situation. Over the following twelve months we never looked back. We pulled ourselves back from the brink of financial disaster and, as always, our garden continued to draw large numbers of visitors!

CHAPTER ELEVEN

Having learnt a very painful and costly lesson, it was obvious to me that I would now have to try to become more psychically self-sufficient. But self-confidence is not achieved overnight. I felt I really needed more evidence from William Thomas if I was to cement the trust between us and I required something to build that trust. Why was this parson, who lived on a Dorset estate so long ago, interested in me now?

When William Thomas had first communicated with us in 1983 I had merely listened to what he had to say. I did not feel it right to question him in any way as it seemed somewhat disrespectful. I did not like to appear distrusting, especially of a cleric, be he dead or alive. But I was now beginning to understand that I did not need to 'ask' questions. All that was necessary was for me to 'think' them. So once again I asked Eve to work for us and, as always, she willingly agreed. Again the results were very good and the communication served to explain several areas within my own memory that had concerned me for years, but for which I had never had a satisfactory explanation. On this occasion I was to find out firstly just why I had been aware of a vicar watching me as a child and secondly why, when I first married, I was visited with faint memories of a grand life-style. The answers lay in the following transcript. William Thomas starts off by greeting Brian and then turns his remarks towards me.

'I bid you welcome Sir, it is good to greet a young friend once again. You have had your arms well filled with much mud in the last few months have you not? You have worked on some most difficult sites. It has its benefits I suppose, although I must admit that it is not industry that I would care to partake of, so I admire you my young friend for having the courage to stick with such a difficult physical task. The day will come when you will score, have not fear. Though,

at present, it may be a little difficult and your purse strings are pulled tighter than you would like, these days are good for you for they will teach you to be a little more responsible when the jewels of the future, once again, unfold before you. These difficult days will not last forever, though you will struggle for some time yet.'

Then, addressing me: *'I have heard you asking a question. You wanted to know if you were the daughter of the old hag who resided in this cottage. The answer is most definitely not. You belong to the big house, not to the small one. Amongst five daughters you would find yourself. That will give you something else to go searching the records for. But you are there, sitting in the centre of five girls. You know that, once again, you will start tearing the garden about and it is good that, at long last, you are using a measure of practical common sense to work out the difference between measurements of my time and those of your day and age.*

The horses still hide secrets beneath their hooves but unfortunately they are not for you to find. The site they cover up is of such antiquity that I doubt if anybody has the knowledge to recognize what is there any longer. The dolts and fools, who would tear up that land, can see no further than their eyes and their purse strings can take them. That is their loss and your gain for still, on the boundary lines, lies the fringes of a fascinating tale which goes back before the Roman invaders. So I taught in my day, for it was my will and delight also to spend many hours searching ancient records and other avenues which brought to light many secrets of the past. It is those energies that I share with my young friends today. The stories of the past that I have given to you about the Celts, who dwelt hereabouts many centuries ago, was real and the evidence lies still in the ground, though there is little chance that much of it will ever be found. From time to time, possibly, one or two small trinkets will float near enough to be found by those who have true inner sight into such matters.

Around your neck, at one time, lay a strand of wondrous sparkling pearls. They fully startled the eyesight with their beauty and with their many sparkling colours, as the lights in the ballroom played upon them. They lay on a most beautiful milky white neck. In those days you were my favourite but I never told your sisters for that would not have been right. And so the bond between the two of us was made which has never been broken.

I continued to be interested in your life from that bond of faith and love that was struck between a maid and a cleric in this county of Dorset so long ago. You wondered why a tale of your property has unfolded so and what part I have played in its history. Now you know. I was already reaching a senior age when you were in the brightness of youth and there was, within you even at that age, a special quality which could not be liberated by one lifetime upon earth.'

Needless to say, following this communication I was off, once again, to search the records. William Thomas had said I had been the middle of five daughters in the family, who resided in the estate house, when he was the rector. The records confirmed that there were five daughters. Another point of great interest, that I was able to find out from these same records, was that this middle daughter had, after marriage, gone to live in Somerset. At a later date, my researcher, John, took me to visit the estate on which she had lived as a married woman. The reader will, perhaps, remember that on my first visit to Eve, at her flat in Bournemouth long before any trance communication work was attempted, she had described a lady, from the past, who lived in a country house in Somerset. Eve had said this lady had a strong connection with me. It now appears that, at that time, she was picking up on my past incarnation as Catherine Uvedale of Long Crichel in Dorset who married into the then Preston family of Cricket St. Thomas, in Somerset.

I found it all rather astonishing. I could not deny that I had been aware of a clergyman watching over me as a child. I was also well aware now that many young children are visually very psychic and that would explain why I could see him then but not now. Also there is no denying that I had been having recollections of a rather grand life-style long before I met Eve. However, there were still some unanswered questions. The main one was my attachment to this piece of land. William Thomas had told Brian and me that we had lived on the cottage site around 3000BC. He had also told me of a life, lived nearby some four hundred years ago, and I had been able to back up these facts by searching the local historic records. I certainly would not be able to prove a life in 3000BC by searching records. Was I to accept this without questions merely because I had been able to prove the validity of the other information I had been given?

Surprisingly I was to receive confirmation of the information that related to my life on that site around 3000BC. The reader may recall one of our earlier communications from William Thomas, in which he said:

'We know that you would unlock time but the area that you would unlock has a special seal. There is only one who is capable of breaking that seal. The day that he comes here you will find the deeper evidence – we have only been permitted to part with some knowledge of these facts.'

In January 1986 the healer Cyril, who had helped us with some of the early trance experiments, put us in touch with Bob Sephton, a dowser of earth energies. The particular field in which Bob specialised was dowsing for natural energy fields and, in many cases, rebalancing and readjusting them, particularly for people who were adversely affected by their influence. As a result of this meeting, Bob was asked by Cyril if he would be interested in making some dowsing investigations around the area of our cottage. The reader will have to trust me when I say that Cyril gave absolutely no indication to Bob whatsoever of the psychic history given by William Thomas about our cottage and land. All Bob was told was that we lived in an old cottage,which appeared to show evidence of energy which attracted and, possibly, benefitted people.

One evening Bob telephoned to say that he had been carrying out some map dowsing on the ordnance survey map covering the area of our cottage. The reader will recall, from our experiences with the archaeological dowser, that it is quite normal to dowse from a map before moving on to a site itself. Bob had received some very interesting and unusual results and asked if he might call to see us to discuss his findings and to carry out some site dowsing. We willingly agreed. The information given to us during that first meeting with this dowser of earth energies was quite remarkable. Before I elaborate I should explain that it is possible for a dowser to collect detailed information over the area of his work using a question and answer technique. He asks a direct question, in his mind, which receives a 'yes' or 'no' answer indicated by the reaction of a pendulum he is holding. The trained and experienced dowser knows the answers to his questions from the behaviour of the pendulum. Often a dowser will use a rod, or even bent wires in place of a pendulum. But, in our case, Bob used his pendulum and, from the results he gave us, there was no doubt in our minds that he was the 'breaker of seals' referred to by William Thomas.

Bob told us that I had been a Priestess on the cottage site in the year 3626 B.C. He went on to explain that Brian and I had both been there and were responsible for setting up a stone circle. We had returned again some 2000 years later in 1514 B.C. to make adjustments because so many other stone circles were being formed across the earth. The radiations of energy from these circles were beginning to affect one another and there was a need to balance the system. In modern parlance, the grid system had to be rationalised.

The circle around the cottage site consisted, we were told, of seven inner stones in which the cottage now stood, an outer circle of twenty one stones and a further outer circle of fourteen stones. Eight of these were 'splitters', six were 'directors' and five were 'spirals'. The centre of the circle was in the hallway of the cottage. We were told the site was female and its purpose was one of evidence. Brian and I had returned to this site again, in this time, to make the necessary adjustments because the energy site was not operating correctly. Time was running out for mankind. Energies needed to be rebalanced and the people prepared for the coming of a new spiritual renaissance – the Aquarian Age.

As can be imagined it is not easy to accept blindly the sort of information passed to us by Bob but, we had already received, over three years ago, indications from William Thomas that the site was sacred and dated back to 3000 B.C. He also implied that Brian and I had been 'familiar with these lands' in antiquity. (Chapter Six). Surely this dowser had just given us confirmation, in greater detail this time, of what the Reverend William Thomas had already told us? As I have already stated, Bob knew nothing of our trance communications and when I told him about them later, he was not really interested. That kind of psychic communication had no appeal or interest for him.

As far as I was concerned this information answered several questions. I could not get out of my mind the reaction I experienced on that day when the mechanical excavator started its dreadful work of desecration in the adjoining field. I did, indeed, have some deep affinity with this piece of land which I could not deny. From the day Brian and I had first come to the cottage we felt we had 'come home'. (Chapter 3) We were continually aware of the 'pull' in the solar plexus, whenever we travelled away from the cottage. (Chapter 4) And, further back, in my childhood, there was that feeling that I was to prepare myself for something that was to be done in the future. (Introduction)

Now we were really beginning to understand the depth and complexity of our situation. In many ways it was a great relief to have reached this stage. We had no choice but to accept our circumstances, though it was still difficult to surrender ourselves entirely to the intuitive promptings that beset us. It was a particularly interesting situation because it seemed to emphasise the degree of self-will that was always ours. We were always free to ignore the influences that were coming through. Through our experiences, our growing knowledge, we had begun to trust, to have faith. But, there is a world of difference between having faith in what someone else tells you and what you have learned from within.

How difficult it is for the citizens of today to hear that small inner voice. Without it, all we hear is the cacophony of the modern world – a thousand leaders saying do this, – do that, – until we decide to move in the direction of the loudest voice instead of the quietest. It is that still, small voice which has increasingly commanded my respect and attention over the years. I discovered that there is another part of me beside the one that gets on with everyday living. It was not as though I had ever had hours to spend day-dreaming, since I have always lived a very busy and active life and yet, within every day, there would be some time when my mind would roam into distant realms of thought. Time spent in this inner land was always totally engaging and satisfying.

Bob told us that adjustments were necessary – the earth energy needed rebalancing. We asked if he would do this for us and he agreed. He was, without doubt, the person to carry out such an operation. We had been told of his coming and had to assume there was some far distant connection between him and us. I must emphasise here that, apart from his natural dowsing ability and knowledge in a particular field of dowsing, he was a scientist and engineer working in the energy production industry and particularly well-equipped to work out the complicated calculations required to rebalance the site. I fear I am not able to explain, in any detail, exactly what he did. Dowsing was not the only skill involved. It took several months of calculation and preparation and an awful lot of paper. It involved not only our cottage site but several of the well known sacred energy sites in Dorset. The correct month, day and time were set for the re-introduction of the energy to the rebalanced site around the time of the new moon and a small ceremony of dedication was held. Our site was now in perfect balance and in total harmony with other similar sites. We had, as far as we could see, completed what we had set out to do in this lifetime on that site. In many ways it was a great relief. If we had achieved nothing else on this land we had left it rebalanced for the greater benefit of humanity.

I have to admit that I was, at first, somewhat bemused by the idea of 'site rebalancing'. But, as so often happens when working in the psychic field, I started to come across other reports of incidents which all seemed to point in the same direction and emphasise the attention and effort being given to 'energy sites' today. This work was quite beyond the capability Brian and I had developed in this lifetime. However we had, by trial and error and not a little guidance, arrived at the right place at the right time in order to find the right person to effect the right adjustments. We felt in awe of the task we had completed. Now that it was over we sensed a feeling of anticipation. What next?

CHAPTER TWELVE

As I move towards the next part of my story of life at the cottage the reader will find us, yet again, having to come to terms with deeper realities than those to which we were accustomed. What we thought might be necessary or desirable in worldly life did not apply from the inner or spiritual point of view. The conflict between material desires and inner wisdom can produce some very painful lessons, but the rewards lie in increased strength and confidence and an ever-developing understanding. The way to achievement lies in letting go and trusting the future.

During this period of growth I received a lot of practical help and encouragement. I started to develop my own skills in psychic communication and it is the story of this development that forms the next part of my tale.

We found it difficult to ignore the apparent coincidences that brought us together with certain people. I suspect it was more than coincidence – rather the gentle prodding of intuitive forces. I receive these more and more clearly as the years go by.

By 1987 Brian and I had reached the stage of classing our friends and acquaintances as those who knew the 'real' us and those who knew only the 'worldly' us. It was a strange situation and difficult to handle at times. To make what were apparently worldly decisions, simply after consulting our inner knowledge produced actions and behaviour that sometimes seemed a bit strange to those friends who did not know the full story.

We wanted to tell our closer friends and sometimes tried but after a few unsuccessful attempts, we gave up. We had taken a long time to reach a level of knowledge and understanding and that could not be explained in a few minutes. They were politely attentive but we could feel that their credulity had been stretched beyond the bounds of friendship. We were either daft, very naive, or on some ego trip. One or two of them were prepared to concede that there might be something in it as we seemed to be, in all other respects, quite normal. But, sadly, they were wrong about that for we were not normal. We were leading a double life all the time and were longing to 'come out'. Even among the group of psychic friends, with whom we were associating, we felt restricted. We needed to mix with people with wider interests, with people who not only had their heads in the clouds but also had their feet firmly on the ground. We needed some sort of intellectual link with our spirituality. The next move was set up for us.

Ronnie, a friend I had made through my craft connections, told me of a house in her village where rather interesting meetings were held each month. She went on to describe how speakers at these meetings dealt with a wide variety of subjects, ranging from say, healing to early Christian philosophy. They covered areas usually avoided by society and from which useful knowledge and ideas could be drawn. It was part of a much wider group called the Wessex Research Group that organised these activities throughout the six counties comprising the ancient kingdom of Wessex.

I was more than interested in what Ronnie had to tell me as it seemed, at last, we might meet up with people whose spiritual interests stemmed not only from psychic experience but also from intellectual interest. Even so it took me a while to muster the courage to tell Ronnie that I was not merely interested in such things myself, but heavily involved. After all, it's not so long ago that such a confession would have brought the hysterical accusation of witchery and an inevitable, slow death by drowning or burning!

It was through the Wessex Research Group that I met my researcher as predicted by William Thomas. After long service in the Marine Commandos, John Lloyd had returned to become a school-master in a Dorset primary school. He has spent hours and hours, over the past years, researching and processing transcripts of tape recorded communication, in an attempt to get some order into events that have occurred. I owe a great deal to this, now, good friend of ours because it was his encouragement that kept me going when I felt, very much, like stopping. It was through him that I managed to widen my circle of sympathetic acquaintances and expand into intellectual and academic areas.

The Wessex Research Group promote themselves as follows: *A co-ordinating network and focus for groups and individuals concerned with new areas of research and experience. We are interested in spiritual, cultural, artistic, historical, ecological and scientific fields. We operate in the belief that there is enormous potential within many people for growth of consciousness, but this is often stultified by the feeling of being alone in their quest, and the active fellowship of like-minded seekers will give them both courage and new areas of search.*

I went on to attend many meetings and lectures held by this organisation. At long last I was not alone. I could now relate my experiences to people who understood and were interested. Following one particular lecture at John's house, I made contact with the speaker as I could see he was 'tuned' into an area of experience similar to mine. This was Harry Johnson. I outlined the situation to him and asked if he could help me. He willingly agreed and spent many hours helping me to break down my cultural barriers in order to gain the confidence which would enable me to communicate with William Thomas directly.

However, before I elaborate on this, I must tell of more worldly events creeping up on our horizon. The housing development around our cottage was becoming far more of a reality. The land adjoining ours had changed ownership, more than once, and full planning consent for housing and roadway construction was imminent.

One early summer's day in 1987, Eve and I were having tea in the garden when she announced that the Colonel, who had once lived in the cottage and who had been the first one to communicate with us through Eve, had a warning for me. (Chapter Five) He explained that when the new development commenced, we were going to experience tremendous problems because of the presence of under-ground water. We were already aware that there were springs in the area and it is worth noting that most ancient religious sites are involved with springs; this being particularly evident in the ancient history of Wessex.

Brian and I gave thought to the Colonel's warning. I had myself heard of cases of old cob cottages, which had no foundations, being badly affected by spring water diverted by new buildings. In view of this and because of the planning permission soon to be granted, I wrote to advise the Planning Authority about the lack of foundations at our cottage and the proximity of all the springs. I pointed out that we had depended on the surrounding field ditching system to control the water over the years. I asked that they pay great attention to future drainage in order to protect our ancient cottage and its well known garden, which was still drawing large numbers of visitors. I also reminded them that it was necessary to divert the footpath from our driveway. My letters were acknowledged and I was assured that everything would be taken care of.

We were very saddened at the thought of all that beautiful farm land around the cottage being eaten up by development. We had dreamed of owning and extending the gardens and increasing our craft venture but such dreams were now becoming more and more remote. It was going to be very difficult to live with the changing environment around our home, particularly as we know knew the land alongside the garden was within the bounds of the ancient stone circles. We could not bear to imagine building on this ancient site but could see no way of preventing it. I could make no public announcement about the site because nobody would have believed me. Had we been able to uncover some worthwhile ancient structure or artefacts, I might have found courage to be more outspoken.

It was about this time that I started to work with Harry in order to develop confidence in my own psychic abilities. I could now see that I was responsible for working out my own problems. It had also become clear that if I were to listen to my inner spiritual guidance, to that still small voice, then I needed help in clearing away an awful lot of mental rubbish, built up over the years. Preconceptions, illusions, delusions, prejudices and beliefs, mostly collected from other people, are like locked doors through which the mind struggles to hear the muffled voice of truth, from the other side.

Harry first asked me if I had ever felt like writing down any of the psychic influences I had experienced. I told him that I had thought about it but had not followed it up. He told me that I should try it as a possible method of communication. The best time for me, to be receptive to this type of writing, was in the early hours of the morning after having slept for some hours. My physical body would then be refreshed, relaxed and my mind uncluttered with the events of the past day and not yet involved in the day to come. He suggested I should set my alarm for three o'clock in the morning.

Finally, the method I adopted was to make a mental note on retiring, that I was ready to make contact. Then I would not be startled from sleep by an alarm clock but would awake when I was ready, if required to do so, when there was an appropriate communication to write down. The result was dramatic. For several nights I awoke in the early hours, feeling wide awake and tremendously hot, which was most unusual for me as I am, by nature, a chilly mortal, very dependent upon woolly clothes and hot water bottles. Normally I sleep like a log, so it is rare for me to wake during a night's sleep. Initially, I was reluctant to rise. I admit to being a little frightened at that stage. However, the waking and heat sensation continued to occur and I decided I could no longer deny these promptings.

I left my bed at 3 a.m., went downstairs, took a pen and pad and sat in an arm chair, made sure the two Old English Sheepdogs were sitting by my sides. At the same time I played Mozart, quietly on headphones because I love music and find it a very good way to disconnect myself from the immediate surroundings. I sat and waited, rather frightened, as I expected the pen to dash across the paper as in the case of automatic writing. Automatic writing is a form of communication where a medium sits with pen in hand, more often than not with eyes closed, and the hand writes uncontrolled by the medium. The speed at which the written word appears on the paper is unnaturally fast and often presented without punctuation. The content of the communication is passed directly from the guide, or communicant, to the hand of the medium. I daresay the principle is closely related to dowsing, in which the hands of the operator appear to react to some independent force. However, this was not to be the mode for me. After about fifteen minutes of quiet music gently relaxing my body, I was aware of a flow of words within my mind. I started to write what I felt. The words flowed and my pen wrote at great speed. My eyes felt almost closed. I was writing by feel rather than vision.

Many of these early written communications contained instructions and encouragement from William Thomas directed towards me as 'trainee' communicator. The most marked, almost physical sensation that I experienced, whilst attempting to write in this way, was that of an immense love being directed towards me. It felt like ecstasy. The depth of feeling I received from William Thomas is almost impossible to put into words. It was a feeling I was able to return after short while. It is like the joining together of souls. It was a truly beautiful experience. I now find it difficult to understand why I should ever have been afraid of it.

Before I give an example of some of this early material, I must relate the following items of information given to me by William Thomas through writing. At a later date the information was confirmed by another medium. He told me that I had been the Mother of my daughter in a lifetime more than one thousand years ago, and he added that we had entered into the same relationship during this incarnation for a specific reason. In 1988, about twelve months after learning this, I visited another medium, Jeanine Glynn, whom I had never seen before. I travelled a considerable distance to see her. I told her absolutely nothing about myself and I gave her a false name and address. I wanted to confuse her because, despite all the direct communication I was receiving, I had still had reservations about the situation. I am not a gullible person and have to be totally convinced before I accept. I think William Thomas was sometimes a little impatient with this attitude but, in view of my strange experiences, I think a little scepticism was not a bad quality to have.

The first statement Jeanine made to me was that I was a writer. I made little comment, saying that I was really a florist. Again she insisted that I was writing a book. She told me the book was not fiction, but true fact and that when the book was published it would sell a great number of copies and would be most appreciated by the American market. She then went on to tell me that, when I wrote, my hand was overshadowed by that of an elderly, scholarly gentleman who had been departed from this world for a considerable time. Two or three years earlier, William Thomas had promised that he would make himself known through another medium, in order to prove himself to me.

Jeanine then said that I would require an illustrator for my book but that I would not have to look far because my own daughter was an illustrator. Then she told me that I had been the Mother of my daughter many years before and that we were back on earth today, as Mother and daughter, for a specific reason. I was told that I would go on to write other books after the first one was published and that my daughter would illustrate them all. At the end of this meeting with Jeanine she told me that my own Father, who had now been dead for three years, was standing beside me, with his brother, urging me to press ahead with my book. Her description of my Father, his brother and their relationship with one another, whilst alive, was remarkably accurate as was her account of their lifelong interest in all matters psychic.

Jeanine had not met my daughter, Lisa, and certainly could not have known that she had completed her four years of art education in the spring of 1986. In the autumn of that year she met David, an army officer and eventually went on to marry him. At the same time Lisa began to work as a freelance illustrator.

In the early days of their relationship it was difficult for Lisa to explain to David what we were all about. She had not been seriously involved with anybody before and so this became a problem we all faced for the first time. What to do when an outsider joined our family on a permanent basis?

Paul, who was now eighteen, was very much at the stage of loving them and leaving them and so we did not, as yet, have the same problem with him. He was far more gregarious than Lisa and had no intention of sacrificing his freedom yet. For Lisa it was different.

I could never have imagined her having lots of boyfriends. We did our best to tell Lisa's fiancé that we had a great interest in psychic matters but that is where we left it for the time being. Either we, or Lisa, would have to cope with the problems as they occurred. At least we had been honest.

Now, of course, I am a writer and the illustrations throughout this book and upon the front cover are by the hand of my daughter.

CHAPTER THIRTEEN

Here are some extracts from the communications received from the Reverend William Thomas during my inspired writing sessions. The passages are drawn from several longer pieces of writing. Some of what he says appears to be of a personal nature but I have included it here – who is to know what is personal and what is universal? It seems to me that the opening sentences contain a certain poignancy. All my life William Thomas has been waiting and watching over me. Now, at last, he can get through to me and express his feelings and thoughts directly.

'The pen is mightier than the sword. God be with you. It was I who taught you your love of music. I am still here with you, I can see you clearly. I am here by your side now. Give me time, I will show you how to communicate. Think you of that house, I was there with you and sat and talked so much with you in that lovely garden. There, they came and played the music for us. Not as you hear it today. It is good for your soul, did you not know?

Once musical ability was yours, but not in this lifetime. Yes it was the harpsichord, hours and hours of practice. Often it was your punishment for a wrong deed! Music is good for your soul. This is not as you expected. You will get so familiar with my touch. Listen to your soul, your great strength is there. Yes – you will understand what you write, you feel me in your mind and I can read your thoughts. Don't look back at the page keep your mind empty, we shall learn, my dear friend, back together again, by your side so much. The door is a little open these days. I will instruct your thoughts. You must act with a clear mind. We shall remember together the past. The garden, remember the lessons, hedges, tall hedges and the lawn, warm days and the perfume of flowers. Don't doubt, relax your mind. I am not a figment of your imaginations.

Your determination will serve to inspire others. Many will come

and speak with you because of the story you tell. Be careful here.
Always instruct your listeners to find life's answers for themselves.
Yours is a different situation you understand. There has been a great
need for communication through others. Tell people how to sit quietly
and listen to their own souls, how to disconnect themselves from the
pleasures of the world as they see it today. Whilst you live on earth,
I can pass to you information gathered at a higher level, gathered
from many years. So many errors I made in my lifetime as a'man of
the cloth'. Many such men today make the same mistakes as I have
done. The love of our Creator is all embracing. There are no
boundaries or barriers.

The burden is heavy I know, but you chose a life of service and
you so wanted to make amends for the past wrongs. You made a
promise to me and I will help you keep that promise. You will return
this site to its Creator and leave it in trust for the future. Leave it in
the hands of guardians, way into the future.

All are interlinked for a reason. No life is pure chance. The
pattern of creation is a complex situation. Many work at all levels to
achieve a correct balance. Much goes astray. Only those who would
be true to their own souls will not wander from the straight track.
People of earth are not true and honest to themselves. They do as
others would have them do. This is a major fault of the human
race and has been for aeons of time. It is hard for the person of
poverty to look further than the next meal and help to them is of the
greatest importance. They must be given hope and they must pass
this hope on to their offspring. What can life on earth be if there is
no hope or foresight?

You are a willing channel. We can achieve a specialised line of
communication through you. We can pass through you many ideas
for a refreshed outlook and a way of life for others. Religion, as such,
has failed mankind.   A true philosophy for life must take its place.
It will occur over a great period of time - small beginnings.'

Music is of great importance to the masses today. Much can be
achieved through music. Man's mind can be greatly influenced by
music initiated through the right mind. The modern composer has a

great power within his mind. Many are composers in this time for that reason. People are drawn to listen, yet they do not understand the deeper meaning. This is very true of the young. They spend their lives locked into their music. Much is of great use to them. One day Catherine, I shall speak though you, but you need help and training from those of understanding. Others will speak through you. Seek the help of others. You are a willing channel for a particular type of communication.' (I found it intriguing that he should use my 16th century name!)

You grow now in confidence. You begin now to trust again. Seek us more often. There are so many who would communicate with the willing. We can open so many doors for so many, such wealth of knowledge to share with man of earth. Our two worlds should be as one.

Far too much heartbreak is concerned around the death of the physical. Death is but growth, rebirth. For many, after a life of blindness, it comes as a great relief. But so many, here, would be far more at peace if they could see that those who are left behind having a greater understanding. Grieving families greatly retard the progress of the re-born soul. In fact it can cause a total standstill.'

The last statement was confirmed by an incident some two months after the death of my Father in 1986. I had gone to receive healing from a colleague of mine. During the course of the session, I could sense the presence of my Father. He had died of cancer at the age of seventy five, but I saw him fit and robust, looking about forty five years old. I had not fully recovered from his death and he spoke to me quite angrily, telling me to stop visualising him on his death bed. He said he was feeling fit and well and that I was retarding his progress by remembering him as being in poor health. I happily accepted his reprimand and I now feel myself drawn near to him quite often.

I once lost a young friend from cancer. Six months later I started feeling sensations of fear, isolation, and waves of pain in my abdomen. I suddenly realised that I was being 'got at' by this friend and this was her way of telling me that she was dialling my number, so to speak. I then mentally acknowledged her presence – the sensations disappeared and I received a mental message from her regarding her son. She was worried about him and felt that those around him showed a lack of understanding for his present behaviour. I was able to pass the message on to her daughter. I have been aware of my friend a number of times since then but the sensations which were very brief, never returned. I am thankful for that because they were not particularly pleasant. I have already mentioned Paul's pain caused by somebody else's car crash. (Chapter Seven) It seems to me that this initial sensation is quite often used, as a summons, by whoever wishes to make contact.

Now, back to William Thomas:

'You think, Catherine, of animals and you are correct in your thought. Mankind carries a tremendous karmic debt to the animal kingdom. Farming and the slaughter of animals is handled badly. Movement must be made to re-educate and to put compassion into what is, to a certain degree, necessary. Methods are very wrong. It does not have to be so. Mankind will have to think again along new lines and re-approach the problem from a humanitarian viewpoint. Do all you can my child but this is too vast a subject for you to be able to concern yourself with at great length in this lifetime. You will be given the opportunity to work in these fields when you leave this earth. Much can be achieved when you join us again. You will bring with you that desire to work in those realms.

You worry too much about the fulfilment of each day. Time is forever and nothing is ever wasted. All is experience and all is necessary to grow. Time spent in thought is all expansive and if you did not give readily of those amounts of time, then our communication would be impossible. As you would learn another language, so you must learn another discipline.

Life is not really of the physical. It should be also, and greatly so, of the development of the mind. You are growing in your mind, my child – just beginning to experience the power of the great emotion that is at your finger tips. This is an energy which you are all part of. Use it. We are all one in the thought form.

We shall speak tonight about the senses. You have, I know, felt a surge of energy through your senses have you not? Before, they were only partially used. This is true of the people of earth with some exceptions. But, with so many blinds drawn, life's experience is in itself limited. Expansion of the mind by discipline is all enhancing. The great need of sleep is in itself incorrect. Refreshment of the physical body can be achieved in far shorter time scales by the successful release of the mind from the physical body. Heightened sensitivity is the correct aim in such experiences. Barriers can be pushed back and potential increased.'

'The atmosphere of your environment is dense with the energies of the past. A Sensitive can read from these, but human interpretation is limited and poor in most cases. Depth of communication takes time and rightly so. You would find it most strange to walk one day and fly another. Give time for your wings to grow strong. Worry not at the need for solitude for your thoughts. Write of the experience. Others can benefit.'

'In the correct hands and with profound and wise guidance the young mind can be freed and liberated from a lifetime of frustration. Modern day mechanical devices are a great hindrance to the young mind. There is no substitute for question and answer. Mothers should educate their offspring, not leave it to others. This is a serious, damaging and retarding state of affairs. But, to rectify the system, a mass awareness of the true potential of earthly life is essential.'

'Times of stillness are of great importance. To unwind the physical body and free the mind are essential to inner peace and development. The belief that satisfaction and progress can only be achieved by frenzied physical exertion, in the pursuit of worldly riches, is a serious misconception. This state of affairs brings little inner peace, only a shallow and worldly feeling of satisfaction. It has achieved little for the soul. It is, therefore, absolutely essential to attain harmony and balance between physical life and growth and spiritual health and growth. The achieving and maintaining of the perfect state of balance brings, automatically, with it physical health, allowing every atom

of the body structure to find its own point of balance. Therefore, an important area in any young child's development is the training of quiet sitting and peaceful surroundings. A story read to a young child, or the encouragement given to the hearing of the sound of music, would help to nurture this need and desire for peace of mind within every waking day. Children should be trained, and have it explained to them, that this is as essential to their bodily health as their times of rest and sleep. Let them observe how an animal, in its natural state, takes required rest throughout the twenty four hour cycle.

Training is always advantageous at these early stages and also, in the case of adults wishing to re-kindle an inner peace, within group situations. Isolation and loneliness are then removed. Only the more advanced student should seek total solitude for such continual development. This then is today's theme, the necessity to re-kindle peace and the running down of the physical system during the waking hours. The greatest benefit within this practice is achieved when the physical body is itself not tired and not in requirement of sleep.

Music is the most beneficial aid to this state of peace. This is not time wasted. It is of greater importance to the living being than any physical or material achievement. It is a returning to the root fundamentals of human existence. You must not feel guilt at such times. It is a totally desirous situation. Cultivate and develop such practice so that we may achieve great things for the benefit of mankind. Develop this discipline and observe the physical life drop into its planned order.

The energies within the areas of Wessex are powerful. They have their purpose to fulfil. Great undercurrents are rejuvenating and expanding. Their absorbance within the population has a desired effect. The theme of mass reality is difficult to explain, in worldly terms, at present. The depth of worldly reality is little understood. All life is linked into an energy growth and natural balance. You are a small fish in a great ocean of on-going emotional energy: one infinitesimal part of the whole. See, child, the humbleness of your existence. I shall expand when you wish to give of your mind totally. Train yourself, I can teach and explain at great depth given the right facility.

Creativity is in every man. Look to this aspect in the young child and there you will find the foundation upon which to encourage growth of the mind in that young life. Academic faculties will develop naturally throughout education alongside the growth of normal human intellect. However, all academic study can be a very shallow experience if in the inner person, the creative faculty is not also developed. Life, without this personal achievement of inner importance will seem almost worthless to countless numbers causing apathy and a need for escapism with its resultant dangers.

Life is sacred. Every life is of the utmost importance. Too many are brought up under the shadow of repression, feeding into self-doubt, self-loathing and lack of worth. One generation hands these misconceptions on to another. We require a revolution in our idea of reality. But, fear not, for the impossibility of these events, for the necessary minds are entering your world for this sole purpose; enlightened entities, who bring with them an inner knowledge for application in the modern world. Entities of great presence are among you today. Many are waiting their time to follow through upon the next level. The wisely and totally taught young mind grows to a wise and healthy young adult and into a fruitful follow-through of years. A potential of life is then realised and a steadily improving universal situation results; small cogs in the great wheel of existence. What hope I am able to speak of, what pleasure for those who are close to despair at the state of the world.'

I mentioned, earlier in these pages, that I had experienced indistinct memories of a life-style more opulent and gracious than anything I have experienced in this lifetime. My long-suffering husband must, surely, have been irked by my frequent references, in our early marriage, to a standard of living far beyond anything that we reached in our 'suburban semi' on the outskirts of London. In truth, I could not account for this faint, but persistent, 'far memory' of mine until William Thomas reminded me of a previous existence as the middle of five daughters at the 'big house'. It was his complaint about bitter law battles that caused us to connect him with the Uvedale family in Hutchin's History of Dorset. It was there that we found Sir Henry Uvedale had, indeed, had five daughters (as well as six sons) and at the centre of that five was Catherine.

The Uvedales of Long Crichel, near Wimborne, were one of the great landed families of Dorset in the sixteenth century. The family network extended throughout Hampshire, Dorset and Somerset. Court rolls of these counties contain frequent references to numerous law suits, chancery affidavits and contested wills, which appear to indicate that relations, between the various branches of the family, were often strained.

My Father, at the time, Sir Henry Uvedale (if the reader will pardon the presumption) was no exception to this practice and it is interesting to note that in 1597 he was engaged, in dispute, with one William Thomas, Rector of the parish, concerning the income that derived from the great tithes of the Manor of Long Crichel, sometimes called Little Crichel. Uvedale won, but the injustice of the battle still rankled William Thomas four centuries later. This is, presumably, the law suit that he refers to in his communications with me. Some students of psychic studies may be sufficiently intrigued to wonder if William Thomas's early materialistic utterances were deliberate clues to lead us to search in the right direction. Others might conclude that, during the early days of his renewed contact with me – his 'one time' pupil, – the material aspects of his earthly life still seemed to take up much of his concern. In which case, it is only later, maybe, as he begins to realise the difference between his reality and mine, that his priorities become more spiritual, or esoteric.

The Prestons of Somerset had their seat at Cricket St. Thomas, in Somerset and were closely related to the Uvedales. My husband, and kinsman, Christian Preston was executor of my Father's Will, and is mentioned in connection with a number of law contests, after Sir Henry's death in 1599. It would seem that, even in those days, the energy of the law trundled ponderously onward, long after the demise of the life that employed it! The estates, lands and a few local memories remain at Long Crichel and Cricket St. Thomas but, sadly, the big houses were both burned down and replaced and so my own memories of casement windows, lawns and terraces must remain as fuzzy reminders of a far life.

One of those distant memories of times long past was of being brought up as a child (Catherine Uvedale – one of thirteen children) in a different house to the main estate house. Young children were only allowed to live in the big house after a certain age. During the course of writing this book, I contacted the then owner of The Crichel Estate, The Hon. Mary Marten, seeking her permission to mention the estate by name in my writings, to which she graciously agreed. At a later date I wrote to her again expressing my belief that there was another minor house on the estate relating to the times of my life there several centuries prior. I had been unable to trace any records myself and thought perhaps the The Hon. Mary Marten may have knowledge of records I could not access. I received a letter back from her, confirming my suspicions, saying that there had been a second lesser house within walking distance to the main estate house, to the rear of it in fact and inviting us to meet with her so that she show me. Brian and I were excited to accept the invitation and we took with us Bob Sephton, our talented Dowser, who had worked on the stone circle site of our cottage near Wimborne.

The Hon. Mary Marten drove us in her car the short distance to some farm land to the rear of the main estate house, about half a mile away I think, where she understood the site might possibly be. Bob took out his rods and went searching. He began to pick up buried energy indications of an old building. He marked out the boundaries of the outer floor plan with pegs and then ran orange tape around them to attempt to contain the energy of the old building. He located the entrance and invited me to walk through into the enclosed area. I was immediately transported into the interior of the rather dark old timbered house, much dark, panelled woodwork, everything smelling very musty and feeling cold. I sensed a large wide staircase up to the second level, where I found my bedroom and above that a third level where the servants and carers of us children had their rooms.

I was aware that on certain occasions I had been taken into the big estate house as a young child and that it was a somewhat overwhelming affair. Bob called me out through the entrance way after a short while and I found it quite hard to orientate myself back into the sunny summer's day. I remember sitting in a field with cows around afterwards. It was a magical experience for me.

CHAPTER FOURTEEN

After three months of communication from William Thomas with me writing the passages, Harry Johnson suggested that he could help to experiment with other methods of contact. By now, it was not necessary for me to get up in the early hours of the morning to take writing. I could do so at any time provided I could relax properly. Sometimes I would actively seek contact with William Thomas and, at other times, I would just feel the need to sit down and listen as I felt he had something to say. Harry's suggestion was that I should attempt possible regression work through deep meditation combined with some direct voice mediumship.

I produced a considerable amount of material from these experiments using deep mediation to achieve a point of contact and, yet, maintain a measure of self-control. Some of the sessions were very lengthy but all were recorded. Once I had achieved a relaxed state, Harry would begin to question me as to what I was sensing. Each time we attempted this experiment I seemed to adopt the personality of some entity from the past, or sense a past reality. I do not think these entities had any personal connection with me. Their connection was with the site and my observations were objective, viewing them, as it were, from a distance.

In our first session I appeared to be in a space, so far back in time where life reality had absolutely no resemblance of that of today. It just seemed to be all space and communication between beings was by thought form. I then passed to the time of setting up stone circles, in which it appeared that the huge stones were moved by a form of teleportation and sound. Many people will find this difficult to accept and I must admit that I had reservations at first, but I have now come to understand and accept many things which, initially, puzzled me. I appeared to be amongst a large group of people who had been involved with the setting up and marking of such power sites across the world. I was getting indications that many of us were back, on earth again in the present day, to work on the rebalancing and activation of these ancient sites. At this point I was aware that some of the original people were missing and we were trying to contact them in order to encourage them to rejoin us and help complete the task of rebalancing, alignment and activation.

As each session went by I moved nearer and nearer towards the present time. I took on the persona, on one occasion, of a Roman potter who had worked near the actual site of the cottage near Wimborne and I could describe a rather shabby working environment, makeshift buildings, made of timber and skins, and everywhere a lot of mud. I will give here a condensed version of what I told Harry I could sense.

'I worked with other potters making produce for everyday use. The surplus, of which there was quite a lot, was taken down to the sea on long two wheel trailers pulled by animals. My particular job was to make tall vessels for carrying liquids. We built great fires, in holes in the ground, into which we put the vessels, packing the soil around them. We decorated the more important items which were destined for the hierarchy but the more basis items, for everyday use, were left plain. The wares were red brown in colour. I learned the trade from my Father, as a young boy. I was not brought up in these lands. I did not die here. We went back by sea, but in a different direction, coming back to this land at another point of destination. I did not like the sea journeys. There was not much to eat, it was very dirty and everybody was packed in like animals. But I was a craftsman and I had to go where the need was. My pottery is still lying around, scattered everywhere. There are some unbroken pots, lying where we buried our firing kilns, deep down in the ground.

We dug the clay from all around here but the more red coloured clay we used came from further away. The wood came to us on trailers. It was not very good. It was green all the year round and it gave us problems.

There were other craftsmen here. Men worked with leather, making shoes, ropes and equipment for the animals. Metal was in very short supply. All we could do was repair it. We were very self-sufficient. What was not there was improvised. We had animals but lacked fresh grown crops. We had to rely on the people in the country around us. Sometimes we had to take it. We were not welcome. We were intruders. We were spreading our power. My name was Anton.'

At another time I felt the personality of a Roman who appeared to be in charge of a type of outpost away from the main camp. I spoke of coming to the site and setting up a settlement. I said that we had found stone on the site and thus had made use of it to construct our settlement, combining it with timber. The latter was scarce as it was all down at the bottom of the hill, where the main camp was. I seemed to be aware that the site had been a 'magic spot' for the previous inhabitants. I spoke of a large stone slab being erected for the sacrifice of animals as gifts to the Gods. I told of people coming up from the camp at the bottom of the hill, to throw gifts at the foot of this altar or sacrificial stone, as offerings to the Gods in the hope of gaining their protection. Then I spoke of the dishonesty of some of the soldiers, of how they stole some of the offerings meant for the Gods. I was troubled because we had stolen from the Gods, but I had turned a blind eye to what I saw taking place. When the time came for a mass exodus from the site, hundreds of men, women and children and animals moved out and we were unable to keep all the stolen items on our persons, so we buried them deep in the ground. I was sure these items were still there. I wanted to be believed about this because I felt extreme guilt about what we had done.

At the time of these sessions I was aware of the history of the area in which we lived. The strong roman connections had been well researched by local archaeologists. I am aware that I am asking the reader to take a lot on trust, but some of what I have written has yet to be proved. Should discoveries, in the area of the cottage, one day reveal the existence of a Roman out-post, then it will be that much more difficult for the doubting ones to reject my tale.

What we do know is that at the foot of the high ground containing our ancient site with its powerful springs, there once lay a large wooden walled fortress containing half of Vespasian's 2nd Augustan Legion numbering about three thousand men. This camp guarded the crossing of the River Stour near Wimborne and, we may assume, the other half of the legion were inland dealing with the tribal strong points at Badbury Rings, Hod Hill and the other hill forts that threatened the Roman movement around Dorchester and further west.

At one time, I appeared to be a little man, living with a wife in our cottage, in what felt like Victorian times. The cottage seemed to be rather shabby, with pale brown external walls instead of the bright white of the present time. The thatch was grey and tatty. Inside it was dark with few home comforts and only bare boards in the single bedroom above. This was reached by a stairway which was so basic it was little more than a ladder. The man was balding and both he and his wife were short in stature. Their children had grown up and left them. I had the feeling they had gone to Australia. I followed the old lady up the stairs into a bedroom which contained a bed on bare floorboards. A brown cloth or blanket covered the bed. Suddenly I found myself on the bed in the process of giving birth! Harry, sensing my discomfort, urged me forward in time, and I found myself outside talking to the little man about the items he had uncovered in the soil whilst working the land. There were no hedges containing the garden, as in the present time, and I could see across a rough vegetable patch to the adjoining fields.

I feel strongly that this little man was the same one who was described by the development circle members. He was dressed in very rough clothes and wore a brimmed hat. I have the most definite impression that he was from the Victorian era. He gave me details of the landowner of the time, describing the direction in which he had to walk and the time it took him to reach the estate house. Either he, or I, had difficulty in pronouncing the name of the landowner – only the initial sound 'A' kept coming out. Probably it was me who was having the difficulty, as the name was strange to me and I did not then have the confidence to accept any strange words that were coming through. Anyway John Lloyd, my researcher, checked the records and discovered that the cottage had belonged to an estate nearby, owned by one 'Willett Ayde' early in the nineteenth century. This little man also told me how he had uncovered valuable items in the soil of the cottage grounds, as he worked the land. He had been afraid of somebody finding them in his possession and had, therefore, buried them again.

William Thomas spoke through me on several occasions, although I found the process difficult. He gave a considerable description of his life and times. On one occasion even Catherine, myself in my earlier life, spoke through me. All this material felt a little vague, but it must be remembered that that I was only attempting regression and communication at a level of deep meditation and not in a trance state. In truth, I did not feel totally confident that the material coming through had not been tainted by my own personality. My trouble coping with Willett Adye's name was a case in point.

I did not find it easy to accept any form of total takeover and, consequently, found it very difficult to completely let go. I still felt some resistance relating to my religious and cultural upbringing – as I have written prior – old habits die hard! Subsequently, I moved back towards 'inspired writing' as a means of contact with William Thomas as I felt more at ease with my inner feelings. In one of his earlier communications, through Eve, William Thomas had, himself, said:

'I know I can work in a more direct manner but, I am more skilled in manipulation. It is most interesting, at times, to watch my words flow beneath a pen and to watch a mind working away, believing they were its words, when I know they were mine!'

I understood, from this statement, that William Thomas as well, was also more comfortable with written inspiration. At a much later date, when I made a further attempt for direct voice contact from him, I sensed his presence but he did not want to speak and I could feel him willing me to find pen and paper and to put aside the tape recorder.

This is some of the content from those later writings:

'It is not easy to speak when the chosen mode is that of the pen. Our link has been that of telepathy. The mechanism used for a direct voice communication is a total takeover of the personality but this is

only a possibility when the medium used has an intellect that is prepared to surrender to that of another. Some will only link in a telepathic sense. The reason being that the mind of the medium prefers and, in fact, insists on working in unison – a totally shared experience with neither one of the communicators taking total control of the other, two minds blending and working together as opposed to a total surrender.

If two minds are well linked and well matched, in harmony with each other then, in many respects, it is a more truthful and fulfilling mode of communication from both the point of view of the medium and the communicant. This is a very natural method of open mind seeking and influence. It is very safe and suitable for teaching to an initiate. It is not wise to advocate opening oneself to a total take over. It is not a bad thing for the human intellect to remain and feel in control, even though the results are affected by the influence of the human mind. Much of that influence can, in fact come from the aeons of stored knowledge and experience from past life times. You should not always consider that all influence is external.

Have I not said that all should be taught to look internally? The human mind is a great storehouse of knowledge and information, taken from lifetime after lifetime of experience. All are capable of regressing way beyond the point of commencement of one lifetime. In the training of the young initiate, therefore, teach regression of thought towards origins. Look not to exterior means to seek one's answers in life. We must train each to find their knowledge from within. Many turn to external mediums for their answers. Have I not advocated accepting responsibility for oneself? Train everyone to be their own deep source of encouragement and fountain of knowledge. Look not all the time to external teachers.

The trained open mind, in so opening the gate, becomes receptive to the life force fountain of knowledge. All knowledge is out there to be reached for. All are equal and all have equal right to draw upon the fountain of knowledge. I teach and advocate total self-sufficiency. By self-sufficiency I mean opening up the mind and intellect to inspiration and teaching from the universal fountain of knowledge.

There can never be a time when all will be psychic receivers, but all can learn to work from the inside to the outside and not just to operate via external stimulation. All are psychic – most are dormant through lack of use and training. Where do we start? Begin with the very young. Encourage and train that imagination. The most important teachers are the teachers of the infants as they leave their Mothers' arms. Music, painting and physical endeavour are of equal importance to matters academic.'

It is interesting to note the stress that William Thomas lays on the interplay between the mind of the medium and that of the communicator. It is not unusual for a medium to appear to relay accurate information and messages and then to slip into a different style or mode, almost imperceptibly. Those who seek the help of a medium should always be aware of this weakness. What happens is that the balance between the mind of the communicant and the medium, to which William Thomas refers, becomes out of true and the personality of the medium starts to take over the conversation, so to speak. The medium may be quite unaware of this, at first, and then become so used to it so that the communication becomes settled into a corrupt form but without any conscious intent on the part of the medium. This is why William Thomas lays such stress on the importance of 'do-it-yourself' mediumship.

Over the years that William Thomas has been communicating with me I sense a considerable change in his approach. In the early days he appeared quite dogmatic in his statements but, as time passed he pushed me, more and more, to act for myself. It was as if he was trying to show me that I had as much ability to seek out my path, as a result of drawing on past lifetimes and experience, as he did. He has taught me great self-dependency and self-respect and this, surely, is his message for all humanity. We all have great potential, within, if only we seek to draw on it.

By now I was beginning to feel very much more at home in my communication with him. I was confident that there was someone to whom I could reach out to for total unbiased help; someone who would encourage and show me the way to help myself and others who might be interested. William Thomas tells us that everybody has equal right to draw on the 'life force fountain of knowledge'. My own experience tells me this is very true and I feel very strongly, how important it is in this age, that everyone through education and all the other channels of our culture should be encouraged to seek, explore and do everything they can to broaden their horizons.

Everybody, at some time, questions the reason for their lives and especially today when everything is so worldly and materialistic. We tend to measure ourselves by what possessions we have or don't have. But we are all equal in inner possibility and, if we were more concerned with 'being' rather than 'having', how much more joy and peace we would find.

Some will find it easy to ridicule this story, especially those who have been brought up with a strict religious belief. Anticipating such scorn it occurred to me that it would be easier and more peaceful if I kept these experiences to myself. But, William Thomas has helped me see that the point of our lives is that they are part not only of our own development, right through into the far, far future, but the development of everything around us. Loneliness and the pain of sickness, for example, may not appear to benefit the patient in any obvious way but most people will appreciate how understanding and love can grow from looking after somebody who is seriously ill. And, likewise, the patient should be comfortable in allowing those around to help and assist in overcoming the illness or even toward their pathway to death. There is no great virtue in bearing pain alone if someone wishes to share it with you.

In short, our experience is our life. Biographies and tales of travel allow us to experience and learn much from the lives of those who have gone before us. They save us having to do the whole thing ourselves. We can live, vicariously as it were, the lives of many other people through their books and memoirs. With the help of other people it becomes easier for us to find our own way. It is my great hope that this book will provide a light for many who might, otherwise, feel lost.

CHAPTER FIFTEEN

As the months passed we gradually realised that the housing estate, growing up around us, was beginning affect the quality of our life. The quiet and peace of the countryside was no longer to be ours and, painful as the experience might be, we would have to consider leaving the cottage. This would be a very traumatic undertaking. Not only did the situation of the cottage and garden mean so much to us but clearly we had a far deeper and long term attachment to the site. Originally we had moved there by intuition, sensing our attachment to the ancient ground. Now we had been made aware of the reason, only too well, and the link between now and the past had grown strong. But the past is a mirror for the future and the eye should not rest on the glass but pass through it – to the landscapes beyond.

Accepting the inevitable and the idea of leaving the cottage was not easy. Indeed, it was to be a most difficult time in our lives to date. One day, when our anguish was at its height, Eve rang to tell us that she was in touch with William Thomas, even as she spoke on the telephone. She said she was receiving a description from him of the next home to where we were going to move. William Thomas described a house, old, but not as old as our cottage, that was being sold off from the edge of an estate. He said it was set in twenty five acres of ground.

Meanwhile, the water logged condition of the land around us was becoming worse and worse. The developers had started to construct a roadway a hundred yards from our garden, severing many natural springs. As the autumn of 1987 approached, heavy rain caused the springs around us to erupt and the roadway construction seemed to send all the water towards us. The fields directly adjoining our garden became totally waterlogged, unlike anything we had seen in the fifteen years we had lived there. In the adjoining field, which we tried to purchase earlier, we could see three springs bubbling out on the surface of the ground. In the end, we had to resort to legal action in order to get the developers to admit to the chaos they had created. As a result they dug a moat, along two sides of our garden, to cut off the water that, by now, had made the garden feel like a saturated bath sponge. We were very worried about the damage all this water must be doing our cottage. It seemed that the warnings from the long dead colonel were well founded.

As if all this were not enough, we then learned that the ancient right of way, in our driveway, could not be diverted after all. The Local Planners could find no satisfactory alternative route and our driveway would have to be turned into a public path to the adjoining housing estate. It was like living through a nightmare. Our driveway was two hundred and fifty yards long, winding and beautifully land-scaped as an integral part of our garden. We could not bring ourselves to accept surrendering it to tarmac and fences.

Some may think that we should have taken legal action in our fight against encroachment. But, we had already spent a great deal on legal fees during the winter months, battling against the water problems and, even then, we had only achieved short term drainage ditches and no long term solution to our problems. We were fighting a very wealthy, multi-national building consortium with limitless funds and a planning authority that seemed to have distanced themselves from our plight.

We felt trapped. Nobody in their right mind would have wanted to stay and it would have been useless to attempt to sell the property, with all its problems and uncertainties to anybody else, because it had become blighted and uninsurable. We had no option but to try to escape. Our three beautiful horses had already been boarded out at a local farm. Our only option was to ask the local authority to have the cottage, its garden and driveway incorporated within the new housing development. This was the authority's original intention, some five years before, and a situation that we had, at the time, fought hard to avert. By now the unsatisfactory situation was obvious, even to them, so they agreed to ask the developers to make us an offer for the cottage. The developers refused, saying that our situation was not their responsibility.

The mental and physical strain was now starting to take its toll. It was bad enough having to leave, but now we were actually begging to have the cottage and its garden destroyed. Words cannot describe the pain endured or the mental battles within. We felt alone and abandoned.

One evening, feeling desperate, I wrote a letter to the directors of the development company. The letter came from the heart and I begged them to review our position from a humanitarian point of view. They were in a position to give us our freedom and I appealed to them to do so. They agreed to reconsider and then a few days later refused again to negotiate. I felt emotionally broken.

Unknown to me, at that time, my Mother had consulted with a medium for her own personal reasons. At that meeting my Mother was given a message for me from my dead Father. My Mother was not aware of our precarious situation or my emotionally low state and so did not understand the message my Father had for me. He told me that all was not lost yet. He advised me to telephone one of the directors of the development company, who I knew was slightly older and a little softer than some of his younger colleagues, and ask him to encourage his fellow directors once again to consider negotiating with us. My Father assured me the result would be positive. I responded accordingly and the door to communication was open once again. Following weeks of delicate and painful negotiation, we finally settled on a sale figure. At last we could afford to move and I had received graphic evidence of how close those who care for us, in other realities, can help us if we are open to the possibility.

During this time of great trauma, there was one bright spot. As the developers carried out their roadway construction, the excavation uncovered a Roman military road, the course of which ran through the field next to our garden. Eve had told us we were on an ancient travelling route. We had never guessed just how close. Now it seemed likely that the stories of artefacts and trinkets beneath the surface were true, though probably they were at a deep level. But artefacts and trinkets, even treasures, did not seem important any more. We now understood our relationship with the land. The energy site had been rebalanced for the approaching Aquarian Age and we had to assume that we had achieved all we had come there to do. What had been balanced in the physical now had been balanced in the etheric dimension. The rebalancing of the site, with the emanations of all that had happened on and around it had been recorded. Nothing could erase them.

Some readers may still have difficulty understanding the principles involved in earth energy balancing and to those, I would say that the fact that you are reading this book means that, at least, you are curious and desire to broaden your horizon. That is a valuable gift in itself. As the years go by, your understanding will broaden and you will be surprised that you ever had difficulties with the new Aquarian dimensions.

As we struggled through this most difficult of times, William Thomas inspired us and I would like to share some of his utterances, communicated to me using the writing technique. To make the decision to abandon the site required much soul searching but William Thomas gave all the assistance he could whilst leaving the final decision to us. Though some of his remarks are addressed to me, personally, I have included them as they are relevant, in one way or another, to everyone.

Responsibility for personal development:

'Freedom is your entitlement. Move forward in your search of the self. Examine your mind today. If space and peace is what your inner being desires, then seek that path, for that is where you will best experience that inner growth.

No experience is ever wasted. It is part of the learning process, equipping your intellect for the tasks ahead.

Follow those strong inner desires. The days of uncertainty and dependence on others have been left far behind. You know now that you need look to no man for your path in this lifetime.

We owe nothing to any man. No human should be chained to another human or to events. If your forward expansion is not to the detriment of others, then feel free. Your responsibilities to others must be closely examined. Let not any man lean on the shoulder of another and restrict his progress. Does he not then deny the right of that person to grow unhindered?'

Control of our own destiny:

'You have a right to choose your pathway from here. There is always more than one pathway. To take one in place of another must not be considered a mistake. The choice of a new path brings with it many more pathways. You, yourself, have a point of contact as a result of your experiences here. These contacts will continue. Your ability is growing. All experience is worth your attention. We are masters of our own destiny. Yet lack of faith in that ability causes hesitation and retards progress.'

Coping with reality:
'It is the growth of your being that is of the utmost importance. The use of your mental energy is far more expansive than the use of your physical energy. You live in the world of physical reality today and the restrictions of this reality limit your potential. You need not remain chained. You are as free as a bird if that is what you desire to be. Growth and expansion are your right. Breaking down the barriers of convention is a difficult process for a human life to undertake. Regimentation of life, environment, age, all these restrict the free spirit.

You now have in your mind a desired route for this lifetime, that of breaking down the barriers between physical reality and spiritual reality. You have been given much evidence and, now, have the confidence to continue the exploration. Build now upon these foundations. Doors will always open if you wish them to open.'

The continuity of life:
'Your experiences and your writings will serve as a spark to countless others. They will help others to push back their own barriers of reality. Life is not a shallow vessel, but an immense continuum, beyond human comprehension. Many so called wise men have been men of shallow vision, forcing their archaic ideas on the so-called less wise. An animal of the wild has more wisdom than such men. All life is an open ended experience. There is no ending. It is only part of the chain of a continuum. Look not for a conclusion before you start, for it will not come, not at the end of your present lifetime. Surely you must know that?

You yourself have achieved much within the confines of this physical life. It is a touching ground for future growth in other lives. Are you not very different to the person that first entered these lands a few years ago? Have not those years had a profound effect, not only upon you, but upon your whole family and selected friends? Then consider these years as a planned and necessary stopping off place, a stage in your development.'

Children and the quality of life:

'Every child must be taught to understand that his mind is the equal of all who stand around him. No man is less or more important than another, for we all have, within us, the formula for perfection. Sadly, however, we are very often wrongly programmed from the outset. Kindle enlightenment in the right to equality of existence. This right extends, of course, to every living entity, be it plant, man or animal. Human life is not for the purpose of domination, but for the purpose of co-existence. Nurture in the young child a care for plant and animal life. Teaching today distorts the mind and sadly leaves much to be desired.'

CHAPTER SIXTEEN

Our cottage had still not been demolished and we wondered if when the developers excavated that site, they would uncover anything of archaeological interest. For my part, I think it very likely there is something of great interest lying beneath the soil of that Dorset hill. We know that it is the site of several springs, wells and stone circles. We have a plan of a number of very ancient structures – as charted by two dowsers in separate exercises. It is an intriguing thought that someone may confirm that part of the story sometime in the future. However, without any doubt the true treasure of that site was and will always be its energy content!

One day, in the middle of all the anguish of releasing ourselves from the cottage, Brian said he had found just the right home for us advertised in a local Dorset newspaper. On a June day in 1988 he took me to see it. Just one look and we both knew it was right and, just as William Thomas had told us, it was old, but not as old as our cottage and it was being sold off from a small estate. It was set in twenty five acres.

How we actually came to be in a position to buy the old farm-house was a miracle in itself, in those days of frantic house buying and gazumping. Many people wanted to buy it and many had made far higher offers than we could afford. However, the owners, who were selling off this small farm from their estate, were more concerned about who would be coming to live there, rather than the amount of money they could obtain for it. All prospective purchasers were interviewed and we were chosen. We moved there on the first day of October, 1988. We were now deep in Dorset. The ground was beautifully undulating; we had a river running through with water meadows. The views were magnificent and the tranquillity undisturbed. We had received a prediction of owning such a property many, many years prior, when we were still living on the outskirts of London. (Chapter One) We considered ourselves truly blessed after all the anxious times we had been through.

We had brought with us a magnificent bonus. We managed to rescue ten huge lorry loads of plants from that beautiful cottage garden, from the smallest plant to the largest of trees. Taking apart the garden that had taken us so many years to build up was a very painful process, but it felt the proper thing to do. It was a major physical undertaking but it was very successful and, as the spring of 1989 approached, it was clear to see that the greater majority of plant life, lifted from our cottage garden, had survived and it was getting ready to burst into life in its new environment.

We could see the possibility of doing at the farm all that we so much wanted to do at the cottage. This time we had the land, several fine out-buildings and the years ahead of us. We felt in no great rush. There were and are today, in Wessex, a number of 'holistic' centres devoted to the philosophy of the Aquarian Age. Organic farming, psychic and spiritual development and the many healing arts are only some of the studies at the heart of such centres. Only a few years ago such activity would have been considered 'cranky' or eccentric. But, the few were now the many and growing in number all the time. It was our hope that the farm would help, in a similar way, the growth of this spiritual age.

I feel I need to clarify two relevant points. I was told by one psychic friend, as related earlier, (Chapter Nine) that the footpath at the cottage was the 'key to the property'. Having rebalanced the site our task, so to speak, was completed. All the visual psychic activity which my son, in particular, had seen, started to fade after we had made a firm decision to leave. Week by week the signs and the 'feel' of presences faded. By the time we left the cottage the area was virtually devoid of all psychic presence and it felt very peaceful. But, we were still attached to the site and we still found it very difficult to accept our departure. It was the issue of the footpath that, eventually, made us decide to go. It was, in a way, the release mechanism, or 'key', for our departure. As I left the site, I made the decision to begin to turn my writings into a book, drawing on my years of written documentation of events that had transpired to date. We had left behind our cottage, empty of all our belongings, its gardens stripped – a tragic and forlorn spectacle.

William Thomas was still, very much, with me; a firm stanchion in the curious life that seems to be my lot. His wisdom and guidance are hard to fault.

I would like to close this chapter with a few more extracts of his writings.

'I aspire to write great things to smooth the waters of these troubled times. I can teach mankind to energise itself to cope with worldwide problems that are today manifesting themselves. Famine, flood and disease are all here to serve their allotted purpose. They are the learning ground of human perception. We are what we create and we can turn the tide of change if we so believe.

There is a group of highly evolved souls. You would understand them to be guardians or watchers who look over mankind and the environment. Their influence is among your world leaders today. There are people in high office today who have elected so to be and this is because they are receptive to the influence of these guardians.

All can aspire to the guiding influence providing they do not adhere to in-built dogmas. An uninhibited search for the truth is the only clear course towards such unity of purpose between man of earth and the thought powers of other realms.

I have spoken before about musicians, artists and writers. Because of the receptiveness of the artistic mind, they are very often magnificent channels for receiving influence from higher realms of thought. This influence can then pass through their work to others, who are less receptive to such thought energy. Look to your artists for the light to life.

Cast aside old mind patterns and remove all limits, dogmas and creeds. Become as free as was the earliest of earth's inhabitants. You are all energy. Your mind is your most dynamic piece of equipment.

Life upon earth is a gift and a challenge. When the numbers increase among mankind who understand their reason for being here, then shall there start to show great improvement in the worldwide situations. It is important, therefore, that we make every effort to light the spark within as many as we can possibley reach in one person's lifetime. Spread the word and pass all I can give you on to others. Other communicating minds are doing the same, this you are aware of. You and I are but a pair among so many. We all have our part to play in our particular area of authority. Some by their very nature have to work in a subtle way, others, with more flamboyant person-alities, can achieve more dynamic results. However, both approaches are of equal importance because different people are, of course, affected by different modes of approach. Some are not impressed by sensationalism while, for others, this is the only way to dent their walls of rigid thought.

Growth of human form is a learning of the inner self. We are all capable of solving our problems, both internal and external, by looking deep within our beings. The human form is unique and developed to be totally self-sufficient and self-rejuvenating, if only we give it the space, time and peace so to do. We turn too much to artificial aids to support human life and, in so doing, cut off and deem useless the body's inbuilt abilities. We must instruct the human race to rekindle those abilities, so powerful, within our predecessors. Time was when there were no artificial aids, then man was truly self-sufficient in body and mind. Because of the total lack of self-dependence today, man feels inadequate and cannot relate to the reality he has to endure. Escape routes are searched for, despair is most prevalent today.

There is insufficient time for peace and self-appraisal within the hustle of modern technological life today. Do not surrender your intellect to machines, they are without souls. Man must interrelate with his fellow man. Personal relationships, giving and taking are such an important part of regaining some natural balance. Just as the animal and plant kingdom inter-relate and should, if left undisturbed by man, survive and rejuvenate and rebalance, then so should any man who is not engrossed in external stimulation.'

And a final word to me on mediumship which will apply to many others:

'You have had contact with many mediums over the years. Because of the necessity, the quality you have received, on the whole, has been of a high standard. However, you are only too well aware that even at that standard, you have suffered much pain and confusion as a result of misinterpretation and it was not until you learned this lesson, and made the effort to work on a psychic level for yourself, that the path began to straighten for you.

The moral then is that people must be their own spiritual communicators and not look to others. No human should place their life decisions in the hands of another. Life is a precious gift and not to be taken lightly. It is irresponsible to use one's mediumistic ability to influence another person's life. If one human is aware of his mediumistic ability, then he should use it to help others to dig deep within themselves, for their own.

Thank you.'

CHAPTER SEVENTEEN

Our arrival at the cottage had signalled a gear shift, so to speak, in the movement of our lives. We had come into close contact with energies which, up until then, had been working quietly in the background. The direction of events became more precise and purposeful and, looking back, I notice a particular phenomenon of those times. In coming to terms with the events recorded in this book so far, we often had to turn to people for help. People who would normally have expected payment for the skills and advice they gave to us. But, apart from the normal services of lawyers or estate agents, we were never asked for money and instead received unstinted help and support – quite freely given. Other people have remarked that this seems to be the rule rather than the exception. It is as though there is an atmosphere of sympathy and 'oneness', in which the main aim of like-minded souls is to help others to move 'closer in'. It is also noticeable that, when money becomes the over-riding factor, for instance mediums, healers or evangelical 'media' preachers expecting great profits when exercising their talents, things tend to turn sour. Suspicion and disillusionment become the order of the day. In short, the affairs of man conducted without some form of spiritual base, will cause pain or sorrow to someone.

Through a connection I made with a local healing centre, on 14th April 1989, I received a piece of written information which was contained in an Aquarian Age Newsletter originating from the USA. It disclosed details of an imminent major energy introduction to all major power sites of the world.

A spiritual organisation in Texas had been asked by the 'Ascended Masters' to lead this sacred world event. (I understand The Ascended Masters to be highly evolved souls working in areas of world wide destiny). Besides Houston, which is an important power centre, twelve other sacred places around the planet were to be activated on 16th April 1989.

The Newsletter urged spiritually awakened people to gather at known power sites around the world, on this date, to anchor the higher energies which were to be given to the earth.

Having read this article, Brian, John, my researcher and I came to the conclusion that it had reached us, just in time, for a reason. We made the decision that we would return to the site of our old cottage on that day and, as the article instructed, form a triangle of three people upon that ancient power site to anchor the energies.

To decide to return to the cottage required a degree of emotional courage from Brian and me. We had already been there once since leaving and had found it heartbreaking to look at its state of dereliction. The Sunday morning was damp and misty and, as we approached the cottage up the long driveway, the total devastation of that once beautiful garden and cottage broke my heart. I had to fight back the tears of anger that arose in me. It was now seven months since we had left. The cottage had been totally vandalised and looked sad and unloved. As I gazed upon it, memories of all that had taken place whilst we lived there came flooding back. I could hear the voices of the children and the barking of our playful dogs. I could remember the warm sunny days spent in those once so peaceful surroundings. In an attempt to balance my emotions I fought to remember the hard times experienced there and compared them to our then present peaceful feelings, at our beautiful new farm environment. We had served our purpose on that site and had now moved on to a new stage in our lives. It is so easy, when one looks back, just to remember either all the good times, or all the bad times, but life is always a mix of good and bad. Thinking on these things and gazing at the scene I could also find the good within it all. Amid the dereliction there were still the trees that we had had to leave behind, now in full blossom and the bluebells were still growing out the banks, just as they had been on the first day that we had moved there, sixteen years prior.

We walked around the interior of the cottage. The carpets we had left behind were sodden for there were gaping holes in the thatch and the slates had been removed from the rest of the roof. Vandals had stolen stone from the internal walls, bathroom and kitchen fittings had been smashed, the light fixtures ripped from the ceilings. Water was dripping in every room from broken pipe work and the floors were strewn with rubble.

We knew the centre of the hallway in the cottage to be the centre of the old stone circle. I felt, instinctively, that we should hold hands together there and form a triangle. It was important to anchor down the energies into that ancient site on this significant day for mankind. On the floor, between the three of us, I laid a bunch of bluebells which I had rescued from the garden. The three of us stood there, in silence, lost deep within our own thoughts. I felt immense love for the piece of earth upon which I stood. I now recognised its importance and, in my mind I welcomed the energies drawn down into it. We had rebalanced that site ready for just such an event as was taking place today. It was now ready for the coming of the Aquarian Age and for the energies which were being received through the major earth power sites that would have an influence upon every power site across the world.

As I stood engrossed in my thoughts, I sensed a build up of people around us within the etheric. I could feel as many as thirty people crowding around us and I knew, instinctively, that they had loving connections to the site and the old cottage.

As we stepped outside to leave I realised that the sadness had left me. It seemed uncanny that the building development had not yet commenced, making it possible for us to return, undisturbed, to that ancient site in order to anchor the energies. For that day the site was mine, although I no longer owned it in the worldly sense. Just a few days later I came to hear that the cottage had finally been demolished.

My reader may be curious to know, after all these psychic experiences; do I believe in a God? As a child I believed in Him as a literal and real person, living in heaven, as I had been taught in school and Sunday school, and I said my prayers to Him. I was glad He was there. Today I see God in everything, both good and bad (or what we call bad), or beautiful and ugly (or what we call ugly). To me the word 'God' means a confusion of things, and I don't like to use the word anymore because, for me, it has the limitations of my childhood. Its meaning is confined to what I was taught and makes no allowance for the vastness I have since found. Today I would prefer to use the term 'life force', which seems to be the most common and yet the most accurate one in use today. I know that all life is connected to this life force.

I feel that I have, over the years of experience and exploration, learned to tap into that life force which is both inside and outside of my physical body. I am only now beginning to see the great potential that this life force has – once it is understood and worked with. From the inspiration I have received from William Thomas, it is clear that this force is within everyone, within every animal, within every plant and stone, with the very planet Earth itself and way beyond. Over the aeons we have lost touch with the life force. We catch only vague glimpses of how it was once used, from the few scattered remnants of the indigenous tribes still existing. Our Earthly affairs are in a poor state today but there is an awakening. I am a part of it and now meet many, many other people who are also aware.

Wake up teachers! Wake up priests! Wake up people everywhere!

PART TWO – REVELATION

The Holy Fire – by Michael Berman

Come to me I offer comfort
Prepare yourself for what's to come
The seagulls circle overhead
So take heed of their warning cries

Take your courage now in both hands
And step into the holy fire
Allow yourself to be transformed
In the flames that hold your future

Let go of the past you cling to
Allow the new to take its place
The unknown you've always yearned for

You have lived just half a life
You who tie yourself up in knots
It's time you took your rightful place
And realized your full potential

CHAPTER EIGHTEEN

Four years have now passed by and I feel ready to write again. The reader could be forgiven for thinking that, after all the trauma and excitement of the previous years, life for the Sellers family would now be a beautiful and peaceful experience in a new environment. However, for us that was not to be the case. As the years came and went, inextricably linked to our daily reality, was what appeared to be unfinished business from past lives.

Contained within the following pages are more passages of writing received from the Rev. William Thomas but as the weeks and months passed by he gradually stepped aside to let another personality write through me from time to time. This being I like to call 'The Sage'.

The communicated messages are personal but also universally empowering towards the building of a new spiritual and holistic concept for life on this planet.

We, that is to say, William Thomas, The Sage, and I, write together in the hope that we can re-ignite the magical spark whick exists within the souls of all our readers!

As I have constantly reiterated throughout this story, I have had to come to terms with the fact that I was not encouraged education-ally or culturally to see the truth about human potential during my informative years. Reincarnation is not a part of present day Christian culture and so I was denied knowledge of its existence. In order to conform with this indoctrination, as I see it, I was obliged to deny reincarnation. This was difficult because a part of me knew it has validity. Such a struggle results in guilt and frustration and the emotions generated are not easy to live with. Continuing to live life according to one's own beliefs, is very difficult against a background of continual contradiction.

It was not until I found the courage to share my spiritual and psychic experiences with others, who had a little more knowledge to hand than I did, that I discovered the early Christians lived quite comfortably with the idea of re-occurring lives. In the fourth century the church hierarchy forbade the concept and it has only been mentioned since by the brave or the foolish! How can a priest exercise power over his flock if their own spiritual knowledge is as great, if not greater than his? What a terrible thing to do, to deny a human life the knowledge of one the greatest truths! Such knowledge is vital if a human is to function completely.

Today we hear politicians despairing about the lack of respect amongst society for one another. They say we need to educate our children in some kind of moral code. Religion for me has made a mockery of itself by doctoring 'the truth'. It is my firm belief that embracement of the possibility of reincarnation into our culture, and all the implications involved, would go a long way towards encouraging a shift in conscience.

Life is a learning experience for us all. It is a process of understanding why situations develop however good or bad they may seem to be, and what personal or spiritual growth we may gain from them. When we enter life, we pass from a dimension of thought to a place of physical experience and we have the ability to think. When we die, we return to that thought place and it is the thoughts we take over with us that are the sum total of our life's experience – the balance sheet, so to speak.

We are not brought up to value the gift of going 'within' to think. This forces us to live life very much on the surface, cutting off a vital part of life's sustenance. As children, we are not encouraged to consider our thoughts to be of any great worth or that our individuality is of any significance. We are given to understand that all knowledge is external to our being and that it can only become available to us via external teachers. As the years have passed I have learned to trust the teacher within, often as the result of painful experience. Peoples of ancient cultures lived and practiced a philosophy of self-knowledge, concerned as much with the Inner Life as it was with the Outer. We, in our Western culture, have lost this perception of life and as a result have cut ourselves off from the universal life force, or God, if you prefer, or that quiet voice of intuition within.

Many people are drawn to study ancient cultures and their practices so that they can rekindle lost knowledge within themselves. However, the mystique of such practices can deter some people and they turn away, unwilling to open themselves to unfamiliar activities. For some who tread the path of exploration, this inner searching can become so disconnected from the reality in which they live, that a separation between the spiritual and the material world begins to take place. When this happens people often feel that they need to change their lifestyle. This can frequently lead to misunderstanding and conflict between people, trying to live alongside one another, but with completely different sets of values. In some respects this imbalance is inevitable but, as long as people understand what is happening, it will gradually be possible to have a culture happily balanced between the mysticism of ancient times and the materialism of today.

Though, at times, life has seemed to me to be so confused and often chaotic, I now realise that I would not have had enough experience to write a book like this if it had been otherwise. There is a reason and purpose behind every event in life, good or bad, happy or sad. For me it is the art of understanding this that gives us the key to personal fulfilment and eventual peace of mind, through spiritual growth and understanding. Over the years I have read many books suggesting a particular philosophy and, though I found the ideas attractive, it was not until many years of exploration had passed before I came to a state of 'inner knowing'. Whether I thought an idea good or bad, it seemed to sit in my unconscious memory – waiting to come to the surface as a 'truth'. It is not until a person can reach that state of 'knowing' that they find themselves in control of life rather than at the mercy of it. All of us possess this highly sophisticated guidance system which enables us to overcome cultural blocks that prevent us from achieving our true potential.

Many times in recent years I have turned towards William Thomas for inspiration. I sometimes wonder how I survived, before that link between us was re-established after some four hundred years. As time has passed, however, he has encouraged me, more and more, to look within myself for answers, continually assuring me that everyone has the capability of tapping this universal knowledge source. In advocating self-sufficiency, he was not denying the virtue of seeking knowledge from spiritual beings (or 'discarnate entities' as they are sometimes called). He was encouraging self-sufficiency in personal affairs, implying that each and every one of us really does know what is right for us within our lifetime. I could see that the philosophy I received, by way of answers to telepathically posed questions, were presented as a general formula for all humanity to adopt, in order to achieve successful physical and spiritual lives. I have spoken with many people with great spiritual wisdom and have read communicated or channelled writings from many parts of the world. The underlying theme that they all emphasise is that man must re-establish that ability to communicate with his own subconscious, or super-conscious – that storehouse of personal knowledge and experience within us all. In effect we must aspire to become our own teachers or spiritual communicators.

We are all searching for answers. The world in which we live is torn apart by strife and the environment is in danger of damage beyond the point of no return. We seem to be travelling down the wrong pathways. Some look towards the church for answers. William Thomas has this comment to make on the present state of affairs.

'In the beginning the God Force created the world and man, but the man you look upon today is far removed from the original concept. Many cling to unproven and poorly interpreted scriptures believing their teachings to be infallible. It is not so. Man's future teachings are awaiting dictation. The doors of the receptive minds have to be re-opened. Shuttered minds are the scourge of our time.'

We read in books and hear from the mouths of spiritual sages that we are entering a New Spiritual Age, or Aquarian Age. We have reached a time in the evolution of this planet when man needs to return to the spiritual ground base of his early days.

I have gone within for answers to the many questions and problems in my life. The inspirational replies I have received from William Thomas, although relating to my own experiences and situations are, I feel, answers that many may be seeking. My understanding is that ancient civilizations were able to operate on a spiritual level with which we have now lost contact. However, the potential is still there and we must simply reactivate those dormant abilities in order to get ourselves out of the mire of confusion.

I know that there are many ancient souls returning to Earth at this time, to be a part of the great transition towards the Aquarian Age, and yet these souls are not experiencing the educational nurturing required to assist their missions. A new born child is an open book and we are damaging the pages of learning because of a lack of knowledge within ourselves and reluctance to change our outlook or even consider, for once, that we don't 'know it all'! Those responsible for the education of our children owe it to themselves, as well as to those in their charge, to be open-minded enough to consider new and less restrictive avenues of teaching for young minds.

Throughout the pages of this part of my book I will seek to share with the reader my own struggle to understand the process and purpose of life. My thought processes have deepened over the years and I question, constantly, the reasons behind each and every action. In times of stress and pain, I become more introverted and the questions become more intense, I sit down, write my questions and await the written inspiration that always seems to follow. There is always a right time for each and every one of us to find the answers. For my own part, I know it has become a case of 'seek and ye shall find'. Sometimes we are not ready to ask questions. It is just a case of getting on with life until perhaps an event occurs and causes us to question more deeply than before. The important and most sustaining fact I have learned is that, although life may be physically and mentally difficult to bear at times, there is a definite purpose to it. Life always goes on. No situation continues forever. Life has its ups and downs. Learning to cast out fear and to trust in the wisdom of the creative forces is the key to a rich and purposeful future.

CHAPTER NINETEEN

As time went on I began to sense a change in the communication link I had with William Thomas. His presence, within my thoughts when I was writing seemed, at times, to be so distant that I wondered if he was still with me. Previously, whenever his words were passing through my head I could sense the presence of an elderly gentleman with curly thinning white hair, black clothes and a round brimmed black hat and buckled shoes. I was aware of a powerful personality within immense love for me and yet his touch was now becoming so light I could hardly recognise it. One morning I telepathically questioned him on his fading presence. He appeared, in my mind's eye, totally transformed from the clerical figure dressed in black to a being radiating light and dressed in white. The thoughts that I received from him were to the effect that he was changing and growing within his own dimension as I was changing and growing within mine. I heard him say to me:

'You have done this for me as I have for you. Our connection was achieved and as a result we have both grown and advanced and are now both ready to move on to greater things.'

At that moment I felt a significant wave pass through me. He went on to say:

'There are now many who surround you, child, for there are so many beings who would seek a bright light. Trust yourself; your inner emotions are your monitor and judge of good over evil. Take the skills of your endeavours and step further day by day and see where they shall lead you upon a pathway of education of your fellow man as well as yourself. The programme is within you, awaiting activation.

I have served my purpose, child, by your side. We have grown in stature together, you in your reality and me within mine. I shall stand aside of your being. You have no need of my protection now, for you have your own inner awareness and understand the depth of your knowledge and experience. You are who you are, who you have been and who you shall be in the future. My love and life is with you, child. God be with you.'

At that point I felt overwhelmed with a sense of loss – as if I had lost a devoted Father. Almost immediately further words poured into my mind but the personality around me now felt detached and unfamiliar. The source of my inspiration had changed and from that moment onwards the passages of writing came to me from a different entity.

The feeling that came over me, as I sat to write, was that of a being of great self-control, wisdom and dignity. Instead of one personality, he produced many different faces. Indeed, he told me that he has had many lives, in many guises, and that he draws wisdom from each and every life experience as required. He added that this gift is available to us all. He told me that I can place whatever face upon him that I feel most comfortable with on any chosen day, because it is only human form that feels the need to place a face and name to an energy. I felt great respect for this personality, as though I was a pupil of a great teacher, and I was sure I would grow in knowledge with him. The following passage of writing, describing his relationship to me, was offered early in January of 1992.

'I am a man of profound wisdom and knowledge and yet it belongs not to me but to the myriads of life experiences that I have been. No man is an island, he is but a pebble upon the shore of humanity, once a part of a whole stone, now in this time in evolution, just a small pebble, but within that pebble lies memory of connection to all the pebbles that surround and of which it was once a part. We are all one, we have been apart but we shall all unite in spiritual reunion, this time so much wiser for our individual experiences.

I seek not to teach but to offer you my hand as a friend to support you to teach yourself from the interior knowledge of your very being, for the knowledge is within you as it is with me. It is within your fellow men, they just fail to recognise the depth of their beings. Be as your being tells you and you shall not miss your life's pathway.

Be true firstly to yourself and be not as others would have you be. Your conscience is your guardian angel - ignore it at your own peril. It is to yourself and yourself alone that you have to answer. Remember this, child, and teach of this wisely to your fellow man. Advocate self-sufficiency among your fellow travellers. For life is a lone journey, but we can seek fellow travellers to be our companions.'

Early in 1992 I had the opportunity of meeting a talented medium, Bobby Simpson, and whilst I was talking with her, she began to describe a guide figure she sensed was working with me. She found his presentation to her confusing. One moment he appeared as a Chinese gentleman, the next moment he was wearing a saffron robe. He was showing her the diversity that he had explained to me and I found it most reassuring to have this confirmation of his presence.

From time to time I still felt the presence of William Thomas – often when I was out walking the fields with the dogs. He still brought much warmth to me and he spoke words of immense encouragement within my mind, especially if I was feeling at a low point, or conversely, when I was feeling happy with life. As I was walking along, with my mind far away, I would suddenly become aware of someone singing hymns very loudly and robustly in my head and I knew it was him making his presence felt. The hymns became a sort of signature and it always made me smile.

I now had another source of wisdom at my finger tips. Why should it be that this was a gift for me in this lifetime? Maybe it is because I am an inquisitive type of person who has always desired fresh pastures, urged on by interesting spiritual and psychic discoveries. Seek and ye shall find! I do realise that because I have always wanted to push forward I have, at times, made life very difficult or challenging. This is a way of life I have shared with Brian, who appears to have the same inner drive. We learn from taking on challenges. Sometimes it seems, in the worldly sense, that we have failed a challenge. However, my spiritual education, at the hands of my discarnate friends, has shown me that there is no such thing as failure. All life is an experience, an exploration and chance to learn and grow. The only failure is if we don't learn from our experience. Whether we consider the experience to be good or bad is not the important issue.

I know that it is because of a challenging life experience that I have been forced to search, firstly within my own mind for strength and understanding and secondly across far greater horizons of possibility. Without access to this self-help system, which I know we all have, I probably would not have been able to cope with some of the situations in which I have placed myself. When things get tough, I go within and there I find strength. It took me a long time to re-discover this amazing quality, which I know we all possess. I will now quote some of the teachings I received from The Sage.

Searching the pathway:
'Along the myriads of lanes and pathways of future life lie many challenges, necessitating you to seek your directives and answers from a deeper and deeper level of consciousness. Wisdom that lies deep within the apple, for as yet, you have only removed the skin and the succulence of the wisdom of the fruit lies deep.

Many are wandering within the realms of humanistic fog. Sit quiet and alone, feel connected to all. Grains of wisdom drop towards earth and await the rains of human desire to activate their growth. Faith is skin deep; knowing has its roots deep within the earth. Seek roots of great depth.'

Thought:
'Look not at the surface of the day, but to the thoughts that day has left you with. It is the thoughts that have the message of learning contained within them. Thought is your monitor, thought is with you forever. Thought must bring peace and contentment and if it fails to do so, then the actions that caused those thoughts were at fault. It was wrongfully motivated action as a result of poor quality thought.'

The Maze of life:
'Life is a maze. Paths go forward, they turn back upon themselves, they meet dead ends and we are forced to re-think and start again. You do know, deep within yourself, the correct route through the maze, but the superficial influences of your material life and surface mind wield a great power over the subconscious and so often, the route through the maze gets pushed almost out of reach other than momentary flashes of inspiration.'

Difficult times:
'You tend to consider that if life is difficult, then you are doing something intrinsically wrong, but this is not so. If life is very quiet and smooth, you may well be avoiding issues of development that are important to your being. It is easy to opt for the quiet, safe and undisturbed life. But what is it doing for the overall education of your soul? Life in human terms is for the purpose of meaningful existence and so I say view not the person in a settled state as being correct and you in a life of turmoil as being wrong. There is no wrong or right, only choice to work at your own pace.

The joy of life is the gaining of knowledge and experience to build a complete picture of your many lives of human existence. It takes courage to abandon the safe, secure and quiet life for one of adventurous experience. Do you have the courage?

Break down the walls of tradition, for they are restrictive and counter-productive. On all levels of life, physical and mental, remove the walls and become a free spirit in your Earth's experience. For you entered Earth aeons of time ago as a free spirit. It is you and your culture that has invented walls, restrictions and rules. There are no rules, only freedom to return to the original joy of conception.'

The Tree of Life:
'Take the symbol of the tree of life. The essential message of continual life and rebirth is the root system of human life and purpose. Many have poorly developed shallow roots. As they incarnate and die, they are forgetting the reason and purpose for each period of life and

death. They lose connection to all the knowledge they have ever had. They don't know why they live and live again. Life is unhappy and unfulfilling. They pass these misconceptions to their offspring. This is like a cancer eating into the sub-conscious memories of your fellow man.'

Change:

'You understand that change can be painful and chaotic. It is not so if handled as a result of peaceful inner consultation and guidance. You are trusting in your own internal map to guide you through the maze of life. That maze you yourself chose to create before birth, as your challenge and experience this time around. Be at peace and take courage.

Scratch not the surface of each day, but reach for the reasons why your pathway must be this way. In every day are indicators as to the ways of your future paths. You can either choose to go with them or to ignore them. Quality of inner life thought gives direction. Lack of inner consultation causes life to be led in any unfulfilled manner, scratching the surface only of every day, thus missing the thoughtful, meaningful indicators that cause us to analyse, to reason and to reach correct conclusions for future pathway projection.

Are you to lead life as a dried and dead leaf from the tree, blown this way and that with no set goal, or are you to lead a life of a purposeful new young shoot, growing upwards to seek the light, feeding from the deep nourishing roots of the Mother tree? Your inner life is the Mother tree. You need daily nourishment from the Mother tree or else life shall be wasted and purposeless.

None shall tell you of your final destination for it is imperative to your own personal growth that you reach it by your own inner driving. You are free. Don't consider yourself to be controlled by anything other than your own free will. All limitations and blocks are within your own mind. There is no such thing as destiny, only a final destination of your own choice and making. You know truly where you want to go. Earnestly and individually seek your own guiding light. Regard life's future transition not as a chore but a joyful and rewarding experience.

Take hold of the life force energy. For so many this power is unrecognised; for others the energy has been dispensed and needs recharging. Reunite with the forgotten knowledge.

At birth the child is still connected by a fine thread of knowing, be it only so delicate in this age. This connection can be broken almost at the point of birth by the use of fanatical scientific and technical interference to the natural process of bonding between the infant and its procreator. If the Mother has no inclination as to her origins, then there is precious little hope for her offspring.

It is essential to mentally commune with a young soul on entry to earth life. The shock between spiritual conception and physical birth, scientifically aided, is destructive to the message of connection to all.

As the blood flows through your veins, then so does the essential message of your connection to all and all you have been. Take a piece of nature within your hand, a stone, a leaf, a handful of soil. Commune with it and try to remember your link, for far in the distance it is there. Take hold of the hand of your Mother again. Relive your life but all times keep hold of that hand and in so doing, you shall never lose sight of your purpose.

When did the spark of inquisitiveness last streak through your mind - when was the last time childhood wonderment brought your world alive? These are the indicators of an opening of the closed mind to the true potential of human life. Seek, for you shall open up to a new and truly amazing aspect of your life. Fear has to be banished. Forget all you have heard about the dangers of delving the realms of the unknown, for the unknown has been your known and is yours by birth right as a human being. Your education and indoctrination has deprived you of your greatest educator and protector and sophisticated guidance system. Your sub-conscious is your dictionary and your encyclopaedia for life and you need to have the pages permanently open to function correctly and totally as a human being.

Your subconscious contains your universal conscience and from the use of this facet, your link with all you perceive becomes one of balance and harmony. Fear surrounds subconscious delving, but ignoring those powerful, life guiding emotions brings chaos and much unhappiness and frustration of non-fulfilment of life for so many.

You would not wish blindness or deafness upon your children, then do not condemn them to a lifetime of non-productive thought or you will teach them to function as a candle without a flame. The thought power connection is the key to interrelated life sequences. It is the thread of intelligence from one lifetime to another.'

CHAPTER TWENTY

Over the years Brian and I have found our greatest problem has been balancing our financial stability with spiritual values. The important sentiment required here is trust, but trust in whom and what? I think that trust must ultimately lie within us. If we are handling life correctly at a spiritual level then this will be reflected in our material life. However, we are, without doubt, living in a time of immense transition, both worldly and spiritually speaking and transition implies change and instability. It is in times like this that, maybe, we have to trust in a power far greater than ourselves – an energy that has already been created and guides us all towards more holistic values as we try to find our ways home.

In 1988 we had managed to buy our beautiful Victorian farm, with many fine outbuildings, picturesque undulating land and its own river flowing through a water meadow. We both had great dreams for this farm and wanted so much to put it to good alternative use. When we first arrived there was an immense amount of renovation required. We worked our way, room by room, through the old farmhouse and converted the outbuildings into craft workshops to let out to local craftsmen. We went on to use one of the buildings to run weekend holistic workshops, inviting knowledgeable people in different areas of endeavour to give the benefit of their experience to others. In between workshop sessions our visitors would walk the land and generally enjoy its beautiful and therapeutic atmosphere. They would mingle with our dogs, cats, horses and chickens and feel the benefit of being among them.

Our dreams went far beyond what we had already created and we hoped that, one day, we would be able to use the rest of the farm for the rehabilitation of rescued horses. From there we hoped to go on to allow people to come and share time with those rescued animals. I had seen such work done before and witnessed the immense mutual benefit to both horse and human. Working with animals in a natural environment enables people to recall long-forgotten knowledge. The resultant healing sows seeds for a fresh approach to life. We both felt so lucky to be living in such a beautiful situation and we wanted to share it with others. It was instinctive to us to feel that we should live in that way.

The year of 1992 was extremely difficult to live through for Brian and myself. Brian had run his landscape design business for the twenty-seven years of our marriage to date and this business had provided us with a good income. However, at that time the country was entering serious recession and, in fact, worldwide recession was a growing problem. Brian's business was starved of contracts and we were losing our main source of income. Banks were hounding small business people as the recession began to bite very hard. Our financial problems were common to many and we could see friends and associates crumbling around us. We were hanging on by our finger tips and, in addition, we were very worried that our vision for the future for our farm was fading into the distance.

We were being pressurised, aggressively, by our bankers to keep within borrowing limits, as were many people with ailing small businesses at that time. A sense of fear was gripping the nation and its institutions. Fear, I know, is such a destructive and negative energy that is difficult to raise one's spirits above it. Fear is the fruit of ignorance and best way we can avoid it is by arming ourselves with knowledge and confidence before the black clouds make their first appearance on the horizon. Thus armed it is possible to visualise an optimistic future, however disastrous the present may seem. It then becomes much easier to let go of the past and allow the future to develop. The world is living through a time of immense change. From the communications I have received, it appears that there is no pre-ordained destiny. The future will be of our own making – according to how we choose to apply the knowledge and wisdom available to us.

I have already mentioned that, whilst I may have all this philosophy at my finger tips, I still have, at times, a great problem in taking it on board, trusting it and working effectively with it. Trust, I am convinced, is the commodity I am trying to harness and this is a problem that affects many people as they explore new ideas concerning what life is really about. Once upon a time this trust used to be called faith. However, I am afraid that what our religious institutions call faith, today, seems to bear little relationship to the trust I am talking about now.

I decided to visit a well-recommended medium during this difficult time. This gentleman gave me a powerful message from my Father relating to the pressure being placed upon us by our bankers. They were, in fact, starving us out of our home. Our bank accounts had been frozen, we were being charged extortionate amounts of interest on top of that, fined on a daily basis, and hounded to place our farm on the market to pay back our bank loan and overdraft. The amount of money we were in debt to the bank for was very small in relationship to the total value of the farm. These were the days prior to credit cards and easy credit generally. We had nowhere to turn for help to tide us over until the economy improved.

My Father was begging me not to let the bank frighten us both into submission and into selling the farm, because he assured us that our son, Paul, who had just started his own business as a blacksmith, was going to be so successful that money would be in abundance in the future. Brian and I were very pleased to hear of this positive prediction for Paul's business. It was obvious that my Father was very sad to see our plight and hoped that by predicting the future, we would try to hold on financially, but we couldn't. In hindsight it is clear to see that his prediction was so accurate and Paul did go on to develop a very successful manufacturing forge.

I have spoken earlier in this chapter about finding the courage to overcome fear. Fear is like a virus. At that time of recession fear caused banks to treat their customers in an inhumane manner. It was a culture of 'dog eat dog'. Small businesses can be the backbone of a nation. These are the creative, risk-taking people that can lead a nation forward with courage. Sadly endemic fear allowed such people to be crushed by the might of 'the system'.

In hindsight it is clear for us both to see that, if we had somehow managed to find a financial way and the courage not to surrender to the pressure of the bank, and remain at that farm, life would have taken a much easier material path forward for us all for many years to come. However, what is the right path, what is the wrong? We understand there is no such thing, just choice to reach a final destination. Do we choose an easy route or a challenging route that may allow greater growth and understanding ultimately?

During that difficult year the two of us became aware, firstly through our own intuition and then with the confirmation of psychics and dowsers, that we were sitting upon powerful earth energies at our farm. The importance of earth energies was something we had come to feel, learn about and appreciate in our previous old thatched cottage. Now there were problems with the flow of energy through the farm towards the local village. Work was carried out by an expert to remedy the blocked energies. This was, once, again, a circumstance that we had encountered in our previous cottage home and so it did not bemuse us. That time it had taken sixteen years of precarious spiritual and psychic experiences to even begin to appreciate that we were dealing with earth energies. On this occasion we were able to recognise and act in a far shorter time scale. This was just as well as it appeared that our stay at the farm was going to be far shorter than we had hoped.

Energy readjustment is such specialised work that I feel it best not to go into detail here. I suggest that the reader looks for suitable books upon the subject. All I can say is that now when I walk upon certain areas of the earth's surface, I can feel that there is a quality of energy emanating that is absent in other areas of land. It feels good to be standing upon such a spot and this sort of feeling encourages me to return, time and again, because it feels beneficial to my being. However, I must warn potential seekers that it is quite possible to experience negative energy which could be harmful in its effect.

Early in the summer of 1992 it became heartbreakingly obvious to us that we were going to have to part with our beautiful farm and visionary dreams for its future. We were offered one, somewhat illegal, way of re-mortgaging the farm, via another institution, but our consciences would not let us consider that route. The selling process, as if to add insult to injury, was tortuous. Recession had turned the property market into a battleground for opportunists, waiting to feed off the ill fortune of others, in financially hard times. Brian and I would have to learn to let go, with grace, and believe that, if our envisaged dream did not come to fruition then there was something else we should be doing. We hoped for inspiration to guide us towards a different path, which, in our depressed state, we could not perceive.

As the months passed, during which time the farm was up for sale, our financial situation became more desperate by the day. We were living hand to mouth and the telephone, that had rung continually over the years offering Brian work, ceased to ring. We were both overcome with an all enveloping desire for freedom from material restrictions and commitments. Despite our love for the old farm, we used to look at the sky and envy the birds their liberty. They were telling us something. We felt like caged animals, unable to function as complete beings under such stress.

We had to apply discipline to our fractured lives, in order to keep sane, and retain belief in our eventual release. We filled the empty working days with walks, horse and cycle rides in order to dissipate the physical energy which had previously been absorbed by our busy working lives. Our dogs could not believe their luck with all those wonderful walks. But those walks, in the peace of the Dorset countryside, served to save our sanity. I sobbed many tears and spent many nights lying awake, gripped by fear at the thought of our eventual plight and that of all our animals. As always, Brian remained strong and resolute that life would eventually become a pleasurable experience again.

I searched for strength and felt guided to study Astrology in far greater detail than ever before. I began to see that the planets really do exert a great power over our lives. There are times to move forward with joy and times of testing and frustration. The planetary energies are very difficult to work against. It is far better to work with them and understand their potency. We choose our entry time (birth) to enable us to work alongside these energies. It took nine tortuous months to sell the farm. But, all the time, the planets were telling us both that we were in one of the greatest character-challenging areas of our life and that freedom would eventually arrive in the spring of 1993. Of course, it did! It was welcomed with open arms. We had survived. We had battled with our minds to remain positive, had been disciplined, held one another up, often with great difficulty and accepted that there had to be a reason for our pain. Thus we had come to some kind of understanding why it was necessary and astrology had helped in this. There are many good books on the subject of astrology and I recommend the reader to explore them.

We felt disorientated when we let go of the farm. We had no idea what or where our future was to be and so decided to find somewhere to rent, rather than rush to buy another home. Miraculously we found the perfect place in which to recover from the trauma – a tiny bungalow set deep within a Dorset country estate. Better still, it was a safe haven for all our animals and, in particular, our three beautiful horses about whose future I had fretted so much. Something or some- body was taking care of us. We may have felt as though we had lost everything, but on reflection, we had gained everything. We were free again and still living within a beautiful environment. We wished for no more. We would rest here for a while, recover and begin to search a future pathway when we felt the need. Peaceful sanity returned and we played with joy our hearts again. The telephone began to ring and Brian's services were in demand once more. We felt in control of our lives, rather than at the mercy of life. The calm after the storm!

Shortly after arriving in our new home I was given, by a friend, an article written by a highly enlightened psychic. He wrote about the many lives that we live and about 'Light Workers'. These are people who have incarnated at this time to assist in the enlightenment of mankind. This inspired article said that some people have reincarnated with the specific intention of going to a particular part of the earth, into which they set a coding in a past lifetime, ready for re-activation at this time of the Aquarian Age transition. Just by arriving on that part of the earth, the coding is activated and in turn stimulates a coding within the Light Worker. Light or energy is released within the earth and the human form that begins to permeate the area. This energy attracts more Light Workers and that part of the earth and surrounding life becomes cleansed.

This knowledge felt like a truth for me. As I have already written, Brian and I had spent sixteen years living on an ancient energy site before reaching the farm. There, with the help of the appropriate experts, we had re-balanced earth energies. At the farm we recognised the need for such work, in a far shorter times scale, because we had learned so much more. Once that work had been achieved we were forced to move on by the effects of the recession, – or was it that? Could it have been that there was more work of such a subtle nature to be done elsewhere and that the recession was simply a circumstance, a knock-on effect, which pushed us forward to a new horizon when, by choice, we would rather have lingered? Maybe events which we view as disruptive and undesirable are, in fact, blessings in disguise prodding us along life's pathway. As I have already mentioned, I have come to understand that there is no such thing as failure provided we can learn from all our experiences – good, bad, happy or sad. We may have lost our farm and dreams, but we learned a lot about ourselves and my plaintive cries for help had evoked many of the inspired passages in the previous chapter. I hope that these writings will assist my fellow travellers.

CHAPTER TWENTY ONE

I have come to understand that there is a relationship between my incarnations and that I have lived many lives, and will probably live again. The reader will recall that my first brushes with past lives were by way of spontaneous memories that drifted into my mind during early married life. When Brian and I were living in a small, modern town house on the outskirts of London, I would often wake up in the morning with the distinct feeling I was in the wrong surroundings and period of time. Memories of life in a grand country house, several hundred years before, floated into my mind. In later years, through my psychic exploration, I came to understand these memories.

Many people are finding the possibility of reincarnation helpful to their understanding of life and through the aid of a correctly trained, spiritually orientated hypnotherapist or psychological therapist it is possible to explore previous lives either in hypnosis or in a deeply relaxed space. Is there any value in this? From my own point of view I have to say that past life regression, in hypnosis, has been one of the most liberating experiences of my life.

Recalling some of my past lives has enabled me to understand why I am here, this time, and why certain emotions seem to motivate my actions. When we enter this life all memory of our previous lives is deliberately wiped out. This is for a very good purpose as it would be very difficult to cope with more than one life at a time. Nevertheless it is possible for emotions from one life to leak into another. If this leakage causes problems then it is best that these emotions are faced and that the troubled individual returns to the past to discover what incidents have caused the problems.

There is a correct time for each and every one of us to accept knowledge of our past lives. It is not something to be played with just because it's there. If it does not feel correct for someone then they should leave it alone and not feel pressurised. If you feel that you are not ready for it, then it is best to wait for a more opportune time. But I would say this – please do not let fear govern your actions. It is important to examine your motives for arriving at your decision. Sleep on it. Over a period of time if you like, but do as you would like and not as others would have you do. We are all at different levels of growth in our individual lives and are entitled to go at our own pace, prompted by intuition.

There have been many very good books written about past life regression and these are worth searching out. To be placed in hypnotic regression is a strange but often pleasant experience. The degree of hypnosis seems very light. The therapist gently talks you into a sleepy disposition, sometimes by telling you to close your eyes and count downwards from one hundred until you feel too drowsy to continue. I find it extremely easy to reach the hypnotic state because I am used to switching off from the outside world so that I can meditate. Once you are relaxed, the therapist starts to ask questions. These usually draw from you a description of such things as surroundings, clothing, footwear, etc and whether you know if you are male or female. I find that the impressions are always instantaneous and vivid and this seems to be the case with most people. It feels like a day-dream, but, at the same time, one has a perfectly clear awareness of one's physical surroundings. However, because you feel so involved with the day-dream you feel detached from the immediate environment. Hypnosis may last for thirty minutes or more and yet, as the therapist brings you back, it feels as if only a few minutes have passed. If the incidents that are recalled are traumatic, the skilled therapist will take the opportunity to help the subject to come to terms with the memories that are causing the damage.

I get the best results if I try to programme myself before going into hypnosis. I mentally request that the lifetime I am going to touch upon will have a relevance to the feelings I carry with me in this life and that I will recognise their significance.

I understand, from personal experience, from speaking to others and from reading books on the subject that groups of people, who have lived together before, often reincarnate around the same time. It would appear an ideal situation for redressing imbalances in the past relationships.

About two years after I had made the first re-connection to the Rev. William Thomas, he informed me, through another medium, that John Lloyd, who has helped for many years now with the research and editing of this book, had been my Father during my life as Catherine Uvedale. I was not too surprised at this as, in many respects, I viewed my relationship with John as a paternal one. I was also advised that Brian had been my brother Edmund during those years. Again it was no surprise. Although Brian is my husband in this life, our relationship has always had many levels. To me he is husband, best friend and brother. John Lloyd, or Sir Henry Uvedale, as he was then, was therefore Father of Brian, then Sir Edmund Uvedale. Again, for Brian this information rang true because he shared my feelings regarding our relationship with John.

Three members of a family, back together again, this time sharing different relationships. Strange or not so strange? It now seems quite logical that, as a family in Dorset all those centuries ago, we led a life that took a lot and gave back very little. This time we seem to be put-ting far more back, instigated by the inner promptings of Catherine Uvedale, who appeared to be far from happy about the way things were handled four hundred years ago. We are helped this time by our telepathic relationship with Rev. William Thomas, who seems to have had a considerable influence upon his pupil Catherine. We understand that there were other members of the Uvedale family living again in Dorset and events are persuading us that this is so. It looks as though there are interesting possibilities developing and I suspect that in time, we will understand the purpose behind this phenomenon.

During a regression experiment that was being carried out as a demonstration for the benefit of others during a workshop situation, I used the method of requesting the experience of a previous incarnation with relevance to this life. While in hypnosis I recalled two separate lives. One was as a North American Indian when I had a wife and young family. I entered this situation at a time when this man was, for some reason, trying to reunite his family. An older relative was involved. Somehow the family had become separated from their tribe, after a conflict, but eventually managed to rejoin it. Life within the tribe was life as it should be led. It felt correct only when led as part of a larger family group. At the end of this memory exploration the therapist took me to the time of death. As a North American Indian I knew that death was but a re-birth so there was no fear, just a gentle acceptance and pleasure at returning home, safe in the knowledge that those left behind were part of the greater family of the tribe and that they would be well cared for. On occasions when I have regressed to life in which the personality had inner knowledge about the continuity of lifetimes, the death process was painless, swift, happy and a release from physical entrapments. On the other hand when I did not have this inner knowledge, I found myself holding back in a body that was no longer capable of supporting life, dragging out the death process, too frightened to accept the inevitable.

The second regression on this occasion related to a lifetime spent as part of a Bedouin tribe. The experience was similar to the previous regression. It again emphasised the larger family unit of the tribe and the care and support that individuals had for each other. They needed each other to survive and did not question or resent this because their lives were necessarily entwined. As I was brought out of hypnosis I knew that it was this element of care for one another, across a broad spectrum of life, that was the powerful message.

Growing within me, in recent years, has been an immense desire to encourage people to be concerned for all life – what today we call Holism. These distant recollections of lives, lived along more caring lines, helped me to understand why I have this growing desire within me. The experiences are intense and powerful. It is the physical detail, colours, temperature changes, the smells and the emotional swings that make them feel so real. These feelings remain after the regression, as clear memories and emotions.

One day I agreed to take part in a regression demonstration at a private function for interested observers. I was feeling slightly uneasy about a public regression but mentally programmed myself to return to a lifetime that would have a relevant message for me and, and at the same time, for those looking on.

I fell into a hypnotic state swiftly and found myself in an ancient eastern setting, angular buildings with no windows, dusty hot streets. I was a man and I was leading a donkey which had large cloths draped on either side of its body. Tied up within those cloths were receptacles used for cooking. I was aware that I made them at my home and was now on a journey for the purpose of selling them. I had left a wife and young family behind. I was finding the heat almost unbearable (in the regressed state) and so the therapist suggested I move on towards night time.

Now I was freezing cold. I was huddled up to my donkey for warmth. I could not leave him and sleep inside a building for fear of having him stolen, along with my wares. I was told to move to the next day. It was hot, dry and so dusty again and, worse still, the village or town I was in was becoming so crowded that I felt very claustrophobic. The therapist asked me why there were so many people. I said that I understood they had come to hear somebody speak. She asked me who it was and I said I was not really sure but that I had heard people talk about this person before. I told her I was not really interested and was going to find a tree to sit under as far away from the crowds as I could find.

This I did and, from that position, I was looking across a slightly rising landscape, towards some small hills with mountains in the distance. The crowds grew denser and denser the higher up the hillside I could see. As my eyes fell upon the tip of this crowd, at the highest point, I was blinded by an immense golden white light that engulfed both them and a minute dot of a figure that stood above them.

At this point I was overwhelmed by immense emotion and tears poured from my eyes in this regressed state. I seemed to hit a point deep in my recognition and memory. I knew I was looking at Christ preaching. My mind was being bombarded by thoughts, memories, emotions and a knowing that all I had rejected, in anger in this life, had an essence of truth and yet had been given to me in a distorted way. Jesus had been a living mortal and I had been alive at that time and seen him in the flesh. Yet, in this lifetime, because of the way the story had been presented to me, I felt driven to shut out that knowledge.

I was then asked to move to the point of death, within that lifetime and I described how I was moving towards that same light that I had witnessed on the hillside earlier in that lifetime. I was aware that my death was not an end, but a continuation, and I was willing to go forward. The whole experience was not one that I would have chosen to go through in public but, I suppose, it had evoked just what I had mentally requested. It was a powerful point of readjustment for my own perception and lively evidence for the onlookers. Since that day I have tried to integrate what I know and understand this time around with a degree of what I was taught about Christ when I was a child. He was. of course, a mystic, seer and a teacher with such charisma that this memory of his time is still spoken about today.

Many, nowadays, speak of experiencing memories of past lives. Maybe it is a feeling of familiarity when we visit a place we have not visited previously in this life. Maybe we meet a stranger and something within us makes us want to embrace them as a long-lost friend. They are all whispers, faint remembrances within the subconscious, reminding us from the depths of our being, reminding us of all that we can tap into and integrate into our present lives. Once accepted, and worked with, the knowledge allows us a more detached view of our present life and gives us the opportunity to be rather more philosophical about problems, fortunes or misfortunes this time around.

After the publication, many years ago of my original book, 'The Return', invitations started to arrive requesting me to speak to small groups of spiritually interested people. Although I thought it was a very good way of 'spreading the word' I wondered how on earth I would ever be able to speak in public. Because of my growing interest in spiritual matters over the years, I had attended many such talks. However in those days I possessed a quiet and retiring nature and, even though I wanted to ask questions of speakers, I could not raise sufficient courage to voice my queries. What hope was there for me to become a confident speaker? I projected this concern towards my unseen helpers and, a few days later, the solution was to arrive by way of an unusual form of spontaneous regression.

I was sitting on the edge of the bath one morning when the thought came into my mind that I should take a visit to Cerne Abbas that very day. Cerne Abbas is an ancient part of Dorset that I had never before visited although it was not far from the farm where we were living. However I rejected the idea, at the time, because I knew that Brian had planned a full day of business paper work and pleasure trips were ruled out. Later that day, when eating lunch in the garden, Brian suddenly announced: 'I think I should take you to visit Cerne Abbas today.'

This was a coincidence which was beyond mere chance. Some people call it synchronicity but, whatever name you put to it, it was for us a purposeful and intuitive incident. Neither of us had been there before and yet we both had received a powerful internal message suggesting the visit.

It was a beautiful summer's afternoon as we drove towards Cerne Abbas. Naturally our first thoughts were to go and view the Giant, carved in the chalk face of the hillside, a symbol of fertility etched into the hill by ancient people. Well, having viewed it, we felt quite unmoved. What next? We studied an Ordnance Survey map to find a footpath or bridleway nearby that we could walk. We could see from the map that the whole area was dotted with ancient earthworks. We selected a walk and drove to the end of the village, parked the car and started to walk uphill.

It was beautiful unspoilt Dorset countryside, abundant with wild flowers and birds. The air was warm and smelt sweet, a perfect English summer's day. We walked along chatting and then both fell silent for a while. Mentally I began to question why I had been directed towards this place on this day. No sooner had I put this question when the answer started to flood into my mind. Somebody seemed to be speaking to me and I was not at all sure who it was. However, in hindsight, I feel it was my own subconscious surfacing. The voice was saying that in a past life I had been Catherine Uvedale of Crichel and Cricket St. Thomas some four hundred years ago. I had accepted this because I had been able to prove the information historically and additionally had experienced a spontaneous recall of that lifetime. I had also been told, by two independent sources, that I had been a Priestess on an ancient stone circle site, where our previous cottage had stood, in the era of 3,000 BC but, because I had not experienced any detailed personal recall of this, I found it difficult to identify with what I had been told. I had not experienced any feelings from those times, possibly because they were so far buried within my subconscious that they were almost impossible to retrieve. In many respects I had also deliberately avoided taking this knowledge on board because I did not want to have delusions of grandeur. This voice was now instructing me to pay attention to the fact that I was once that person and that, deep within me, there was still a facet of that personality. It was the presence, knowledge and realisation of that past personality that I was being urged to draw upon, so that I would regain the inner strength and knowledge that I once had so very long ago.

The strange images I was receiving were powerful and moving. I seemed to be walking along in a dream in which I was being told that I needed to visit the ancient site of Cerne Abbas in order to receive this information. In Chapter Twenty I make mention of such phenomena that require people, within a particular lifetime, to touch on certain areas of the earth so that forgotten knowledge can be recalled. I had said nothing to Brian about these impressions. The view from the crest of the Dorset hills was beautiful, a patchwork of multicoloured undulating fields, their crops swaying gently in the warm summer breeze. We both lay down to bathe in the warm sunlight and tried to absorb the energy we felt must be present within such ancient and undisturbed land. Later, as we were returning down the hill, Brian suddenly told me to stop because he wanted to relate what he was seeing. He said he could see a vision of a lady with long, thick, slightly tatty robes, long hair, much jewellery and carrying a staff covered in jewels. Behind this lady, walking down the hill was a long trail of people following in double file. He said he knew intuitively that the person leading the people was me. I then told him of my impressions on the way up to the top of the hill. We both realised the purpose of our jointly inspired visit to Cerne Abbas.

The visit was an experience I shall never forget and within days, it seemed to have a profound and powerful influence on my personality. I felt myself growing in confidence and self-assurance. I understood the importance of the directive and built on it. The fact that Brian's experience confirmed mine made me realise that this was no figment of my imagination, but a deliberate and important event in my life.

A few weeks later I had to deliver my first talk about the content of my book 'The Return'. I had prepared the talk by making notes. As I began to speak I felt ice cold and terribly nervous but, within minutes, a great heat enveloped me, my notes were discarded and three quarters of an hour seemed to pass as though I had been in a dream. I felt so at home in what I was doing there that evening in front of those people. It was as though I had been waiting all my life to do just as I was doing that night!

Within us all are facets from many past lives. Knowledge from our past is available to us once we know how to unlock the door to the storeroom.

CHAPTER TWENTY TWO

What a rich mix of life and emotions we experienced in that tiny bungalow on the Dorset estate. In past years we had lived in two beautiful and unusual homes that had belonged to us, and now because of unforeseen circumstances we had to rent this tiny home. We had lost much materially but had gained so much more mental and physical freedom. The bungalow was set on high ground with magnificent views over the surrounding landscape. It had large windows in every room and we felt as if we were living outside – the rooms and the landscape became as one. At night we felt we were a part of the sky with the stars and the moon in every room with us.

Freed of the shackles of bank loans, overdrafts and mortgages, we found it far easier to earn our living in those early days but, as the weeks passed by, we began, seriously, to give thought to our longer term future. We were in pretty poor shape financially because we had sold our farm well below its true market value in order to escape the oppressive financial constraints inflicted upon us by our bankers. It had been the base for all our creative activities. We soon began to realise that life had become both a physical and mental challenge and we now had to devise some kind of structure to take us forward. We were both approaching middle age, self-employed and needed to create a pattern to provide for our long term future.

In the first few weeks, after arriving in our new home, our minds shut off from what had taken place. In many ways the mind is such a clever thing. It was as if, in order to let us gain physical and emotional strength, our minds had placed a blanket over our immediate memories. Eventually the truth began to surface, firstly in our dreams. Night after night we kept reliving the events of the last twelve months or so, in graphic detail. Time after time we experienced a nightmare dream of living back on the farm, but living there now with the new owners and having to hide from them all the time. Waking from these dreams and nightmares was always such a great relief. It was as if, in our sleep, we were facing the reality of what had transpired in our lives and were releasing the painful memories and emotions that we had buried in our subconscious. Those memories had been too uncomfortable for our surface minds to handle at that time. In hindsight I can see that the loss of the farm, coming only three short years after the loss of our beautiful cottage to demolition, had left us both emotionally wounded.

Brian continued to work at landscape design although he was beginning to lose interest in his work. It was difficult to run such an enterprise from the tiny bungalow with no outbuildings in which to store the tools of his trade. Missing too was the great asset of the show garden that had been left behind and which had always acted as a magnet for future business and which gave confidence to potential customers. Brian was back on the first rung of the ladder again after twenty or more years' steady climbing.

I began to feel cut off from all that I had ever worked at. No flowers, no craft venture, no holistic project, no vision. I felt at a loss as to what to do. We began to feel like broken people, a reaction felt by so many other people, washed up on the beaches of life following a recession. The experience was more than many could bear. Repossession of homes hit record heights and the bottom fell out of the property market. Marriages failed, families were torn apart and there were many very sad and broken people around.

Two months after moving to the bungalow I decided I would have to improve and diversify my skills. I had spent all my life being self-employed and did not relish the thought of working for somebody else. I enrolled in a part time desktop publishing course at the nearby Further Education College. Feeling like a 'fish out of water' I had to step out of the creative side of my personality, in which I had lived comfortably for so long, and move into the area of logic. At times I felt extremely frustrated at having to work in such a disciplined way, but, gradually, the desktop publishing course required a move into more creative realms and I began to bring the two opposing aspects of my personality together. It had been a challenge and it brought a certain satisfaction. Next, I enrolled on a local authority business training course and, at the end of that, set up my own business to help other authors who wanted to self-publish their books. Over the next couple of years I greatly enjoyed my new occupation and working alongside the other authors I found stimulating.

Three months after moving to the bungalow Brian and I felt that perhaps we should make some kind of official approach to our bankers to express our disgust about the treatment we had received from them during the recession. We didn't expect to get anywhere by taking such action but felt we should at least say we though their actions dishonourable. Our complaint was met with cold dispassion by the bank officials. Banks are powerful organisations, a law unto themselves, and so what chance does the small man have? The temptation to put up with what had taken place, simply put it down to experience, pick up the pieces and get on with life was considerable.

There is a theory that we draw to ourselves the experiences in life that we need in order to grow in understanding. This can be difficult to understand if we seem to draw distressing or unsatisfactory situations upon ourselves. There are many books on the subject of creating our own reality, by changing the deeper thought processes of our own minds with a view to drawing more pleasant situations towards ourselves. However, the subject is deep and there are many levels that need to be explored before it can be put to good use to reveal any kind of logic or explain people's experience of life.

For one thing the subject of karma has to be considered and that, in itself, is another multi levelled subject. We often hear people say: 'I must have done something terribly wrong in the past to deserve what I am living through now!' But the explanation is not nearly as simple as that. How do we measure what is a good or bad, pleasant or unpleasant experience? What is 'good' or what is 'bad' is usually a matter of opinion. So a traumatic experience in this life may, in fact, be a profound learning experience which, depending on the attitude of the personality, can be expanded upon and turned to great advantage either in this life or in a later life. When living through a terrible trauma, the desire to be away from the situation can be so great that one considers suicide. The gift of this particular life experience, or in fact the gift of life itself, becomes undesirable. Nevertheless once the trauma has been overcome, a new kind of inner strength becomes evident. A capacity to cope with adversity is discovered.

There are very few people who would deliberately place themselves in an appalling situation in order to grow in understanding and become aware of their own strengths or weaknesses. I know, from my own point of view that, like most people, I would love a life of joyous fulfilment and yet my life experience has been far from that. Like others, I have experienced very testing times and yet, inside me, there is the feeling that I would not really have had it any other way because the experiences have taught me something about myself and have helped me gain a feeling of inner power. I know that inner strength or power, call it what you will, has, in reality, always been there. We all possess it but are conditioned, during our lives, into believing it is not there. Childhood upbringing, education, religion and culture all mould us into believing that we are powerless in certain situations. I know, from my earlier experiences, that the inner strength or power I am talking about was far more evident in the ancient cultures of this world. The Sage had words of wisdom to on how to regain these gifts. (Chapter 19) It will be the gradual encompassing of such latent inner abilities that will enable us to change, for the better, our relationship with our environment, our fellow creatures and ourselves.

CHAPTER TWENTY THREE

Brian and I were aware that the land upon which our bungalow sat had certain healing energies and, apart from the nightmares and the underlying insecurity, we were both well and happy to be there. We even felt a certain familiarity with the site, as though we had known it of old. So I decided to call in a dowser to measure the energy content of the land. I gave no indication to the dowser of my own suspicions. The dowser advised us that we were, once again, living on the site of crossing ley lines – a point of powerful earth energies. The actual crossing point of the leys was beneath the head of our bed and the dowser advised us, in the interest of peaceful sleep, that it might be better to move the bed elsewhere. He was not surprised when I told him that Brian and I had been experiencing some very powerful and traumatic dreams because the powerful energies would have amplified our dream activity.

We took his advice and moved the bed into a different room. Immediately we noticed a letting-up in the dream experiences. However, in order to take advantage of the cosmic power point, I set up my computer system, used to produce books for other authors, right on that point. In this way I could use the energy for the purpose of spreading knowledge.

All of us can make use of these natural energies, provided we use them unselfishly for the light or in the interest of what is good and light. As ancient beings that is just what we used to do. Needless to say those energies can also be used for negative purposes.

Twelve months after moving to our new home we started to sit in a meditation and psychic development group with three friends. One of these was John Lloyd, my editor and Father of Brian and me some four hundred years ago. John experienced a vast expansion of his own spiritual understanding within that group meditation situation. Also sitting with us were two other people, a husband and wife, whom we had come to know in recent years. Gradually we all came to an understanding of our past relationships with one another. Mary, a working medium for many years, had been Mother to myself and Brian four hundred years previously and was, therefore, John's wife Isabel Uvedale. Her funerery statue graces the church at Witchampton, Dorset. David, a U.F.O. and crop circle investigator had been my husband, Christian Preston all those years ago. In this unusual situation, four members of the Uvedale family and one in-law found themselves back together in Dorset some four hundred years later, working in areas of spiritual investigation and understanding.

One evening, during our group meditation, I had a clear vision of a little red brick cottage that seemed to be on the site of our modern bungalow. I then became aware of a building that would, in the future, be on the same site. It was very futuristic in design, half submerged in the ground and with a transparent dome, just visible. Several months later somebody came to the bungalow selling aerial shots of the area that had been taken many years before, which showed a tiny red brick cottage in the place of our bungalow.

A year after our move to this new home, Brian and I were invited, one evening, to a barbeque at our son's home. The journey involved driving very near to our old farm. Before we set out I gave no thought whatsoever to this fact. As we drew closer to the area of the farm a terrible depression overcame me, but I said nothing to Brian. Throughout the evening I did my best to fight off the depression but, during the journey home, it enveloped me even more forcibly. What I was experiencing was the full force of the sense of loss I felt at being obliged to leave our old farm. However, I could not understand why I should feel so awful on this particular evening. As the reader will appreciate, some years before, we had been obliged to leave our previous old cottage – in even worse circumstances, knowing it would be demolished. Even so I had not felt such intense emotion about that situation. As I went to bed that night, I followed my usual practice and asked those who I know surrounded me in the unseen realms, to help me understand why I should feel this way or, at least, help me to overcome these oppressive feelings by the morning.

I awoke early. Of all days, this was my birthday and yet I felt exceptionally low. I again asked to obtain understanding from my unseen helpers whom I knew were able to help me. I could sense William Thomas saying to me, in my half awake state, words to this effect:

'You have now felt the true depth of the emotions that have laid buried deep within you. You should release these emotions as they will cause you physical discomfort in later life if you do not. I can help you. Whilst you feel this intensity of depression I invite you to write a letter to those bankers,who made life so difficult for you, using this emotion as the driving force. I promise you that, together, we will attempt to win over adversity. You have suffered a great injustice, there has been a Judas!'

When Brian awoke I decided to tell him how awful I had been feeling since the previous evening. I was shocked to find that he had been having a similar experience, but he had kept his thoughts to himself in order not to distress me. I told him of the inspiration I had just received from William Thomas. We decided we would action his suggestion. It took a couple of hours to produce the letter. It was very painful to write and the tears of anguish shed whilst I worked at it left me with little doubt as regards my recent suppression of memories. Once the letter had been produced the acute depression immediately lifted and has never returned.

The letter was sent to the Chairman of the bank and it was to be the beginning of a very protracted legal battle. For some considerable time Brian and I had wondered if it was correct to seek retribution from our bankers for what had transpired. We live in a society, today, where litigation is rife, with the tendency to blame others for our misfortunes.

As mentioned earlier, there is the theory that we draw to us what we deserve, or expect, and thus we should not necessarily attempt to blame others. However, banks are very powerful and customers could be forgiven for feeling disempowered. Brian and I were aware that we had been subjected to an intimidating use of that power. As the legal process began to unfold, the information we uncovered during the process of 'Discovery', confirmed that we were right to fight for justice. Our pleas for help to our Bank Manager, at that time, had been withheld, by him, from Head Office.

I have explained that the Reverend William Thomas, had, in his time, been a considerable legal campaigner himself for the rights of the 'underdog' (Chapter Thirteen). I am no lawyer, but I am well aware of the energy that William Thomas is capable of enthusing me with, when I have to deal with legal matters. I trust him implicitly. It is something that I am happy to go along with. I received from William Thomas many suggestions which were so firm and direct that I considered them almost as commands. It can be an extremely empowering experience. I could feel my mind flying from one idea to another, and found myself rushing to the exact point in my voluminous files to find the pieces of written evidence needed to help form the correct opinion and legal angle to work at when compiling my case.

At times I felt dispirited at the amount of energy I was placing into this legal battle. After all it had only been a few years ago that a similar kind of battle had taken place in our attempt to stave off the loss of our cottage home. William Thomas had played no small part in that event!

My thirst to understand life's experiences causes me to question events carefully. Why another intense legal battle so soon? Was I repeating old patterns, drawing similar situations to myself, not moving forwards? I truly wanted this to be my last legal battle in this particular lifetime. I had had enough. A possible answer to this thought was forthcoming – eventually.

CHAPTER TWENTY FOUR

On a summer's day in 1995 I had arranged to organise a past life regression workshop with a friend of mine, an active and successful hypnotherapist, Diane Egby-Edwards. It was not my intention to participate in the group regressions but merely to witness events. However, as the workshop progressed I decided to take advantage of the opportunity of a regression session to find an answer to the thought that had been bothering me for some time regarding my legal battles. I already knew how to programme myself before the session to obtain an understanding of current events, which might have their roots buried in a previous life. (Chapter Twenty One)

Was there an energy, buried deep in my subconscious, from a past life experience, that caused me to attract legal battles and, in particular, the David and Goliath situations where I seemed to be the underdog, taking on the impossible?

Just before the small group of workshop participants were encouraged to slip into a hypnotic state, I made the following mental statement and requested an understanding.

'I have had enough of legal battles, I don't want any more. I do not enjoy them and resent the time they take up in my life. Please can I understand why they are a part of my life this time and may this understanding help release the energy that is pushing me along this track at present?'

Immediately I was catapulted, mentally, from the tranquil setting of the workshop, on a warm summer's day, to the stinking hold of an ancient wooden ship. This hold was full of people in a state of squalor. I was a young boy of say ten or eleven. It was my job to work among these people, dishing out meagre food rations and attempting to clean up their appalling living conditions. As I have already written, regression can be a powerful tool. My experience was shockingly unpleasant. I was filthy and the air was putrid. What I could see with my eyes was awful and yet, in my heart, I could sense an immense love for these unhappy people in the hold of the ship. I knew they were prisoners on a transportation ship to some colony. Many were there unjustly – being punished for small crimes resulting from the terrible poverty of their lives back home.

Whenever it poured with rain, I had to herd the prisoners up to the deck so that they could take advantage of the chance of a rare wash. It was their only relief from the foul and cramped existence down below and this emphasised the sadness I felt for them. Whilst they enjoyed that small pleasure, I was below decks, trying my best to sweep rivers of human waste out of the hold before their return.

I recalled the homeward journeys amongst the ship's crew, with whom I had little in common. I kept myself to myself. The ship was laden with cargo on the return journeys. After several years at sea, I did not take the return journey to England, but remained in that far away country. I eventually married, and the person that I married then, is my son now!

From that session in hypnosis I speculated that the experience I had just relived may well have been part of the driving force in my legal battle as the underdog today. This past event, the memory of which was buried deep within was giving me an energy, in this life, to put legal injustices right. I truly hoped, that this understanding might mean I had now worked through these frustrated energies and emotions. However, I don't consider that I have to look upon events this time around as a mistake or a wrong pathway. The energies and emotions from the past, locked deep within, have caused me to live my life in a certain way and I feel this is what the interrelationship between each lifetime is about. It is about unfinished business. In other words, my present life experience is part of a giant hologram and, what I am doing today, is related to my past lives and will impinge on what I will be doing in future lives. Who better to assist me in this endeavour than the Reverend William Thomas, who also seemed to be dealing with his own unfinished legal business!

Expanding on this karmic re-enactment theme a little further, it is possible that, four hundred years ago, I was part of the landed family, in Dorset, who were the perpetrators of injustice against the underdog. At that time, William Thomas supported the wronged, the underdogs, in the form of estate tenants in dispute over Tithe Apportionments. Today William Thomas supports me. In other words, this time I am experiencing the 'other side of the coin'. Subsequently during a meditation session I received confirmation that this event had played a major role in shaping my present life situation. During the meditation I saw the figure of a gentleman, in front of me, dressed in legal clothes. His robes were black and he wore a heavy, grey, wavy wig. He was thickset but had a kindly face. He told me that he had defended my family's case in Dorset all those years ago and that he had been successful. He also told me that he was helping me now to expose injustice. He and I are making amends this time around.

These answers and explanations may be incomplete or they might even be inaccurate, but they give an idea of how one lifetime can influence another. To me they are more acceptable, maybe, than some of the ideas from scientists who work only from professionally acceptable evidence. Searching, day by day, for answers about the meaning and purpose of life is expansive and helps to satisfy my curiosity. We all need to open doors in order to grow and move onwards. That, to me, is what the gift of life is about. As children, we are only taught how to live within the confines of physical experience and yet our spiritual experience is, in my opinion, far more relevant. For the children of this world to be only partially educated is a tragedy that needs to be resolved. The long term well-being of this planet and the souls that inhabit it is at stake.

In the three years that we lived in that home the legal proceedings took up a considerable amount of our time and energy. We used the services firstly of the Banking Ombudsman which, though free, is extremely protracted and frustrating and we ended up feeling this system was biased in favour of the banking organisations. Often we felt we were just wasting our time and fighting a hopeless battle. Some friends and associates tried to persuade us to 'throw in the towel' but the sense of injustice was acute and we truly felt we were entitled to justice. To accept such violation is to surrender one's own power to somebody else which, in our particular case, was an uncaring massive corporate organisation. We had the advantage of William Thomas assisting us telepathically with his astute legal mind, and inspiring me whilst I conducted the case via much correspondence. Others are not quite so lucky. If we continued and eventually succeeded then the results would give heart to others who had also fallen victim to a merciless system.

Brian eventually moved away from his landscaping. Our son, Paul, had developed his skills as a blacksmith and was beginning to build up a very successful business, just as my long-dead Father had predicted. (Chapter Twenty) He needed help and Brian, being disenchanted with his own work, decided to join him. There was a renaissance taking place in the field of iron work and our son, coincidentally, or otherwise, found himself, in the right place at the appropriate time!

Paul's business grew and grew. More space was required and so we decided to search for an old farm to rent together where we could both live and run the forge. Eventually the opportunity arrived and in the summer of 1996, whilst Brian on I were on holiday in Portugal, Paul telephoned to say he had found just the right farm. However, we would have to make a decision about moving before we returned, because other people were also interested in the farm. The decision to move was made over the telephone and we moved to the border of Dorset and Somerset just one month later. Joining us was Paul's long term partner Katherine.

The farm was in a truly beautiful environment and it certainly made a wonderful home for all our horses, dogs and cats. Little did we know, in the first few days of being there, that we had walked into the jaws of a spiritual lion. Our family bonds and the depth of our spiritual perceptions were about to be tested to the limit!

CHAPTER TWENTY FIVE

We were well aware that working together and attempting to live under one roof might create problems. We were all used to our own independence, our own space and our patterns of living. Nevertheless we had joined in this venture for a specific purpose – to run the forge, reduce travelling and share a good living environment with the family and our animals.

Brian and I continued to plug away at our monumental legal battle. As already mentioned, the investigation by the Banking Ombudsman drew a total legal blank, so far as we were concerned. After many months the bank was cleared of any misconduct. We could not believe it and the intense sense of injustice still rankled in our hearts. That investigation had cost us nothing other than our time but, if we were to proceed against such fiscal giants again, it was going to cost us heavily. This we could not afford but, somehow, we had to try and obtain justice.

Over the years I had collected the names of a few organisations which help people to tackle injustices in the banking system, these organisations having sprung up as a result of the banks' heavy handed treatment of customers during the recession. One afternoon, not long after moving to our new home I stood in my office and sent out a telepathic message to William Thomas:

'Who do I turn to now?' Very quickly I intuitively knew the best organisation to contact and I was on the telephone immediately.

My call was answered by the gentleman who ran the organisation. He advised me that he had recently taken on the services of a young barrister whom he thought might be able to help Brian and me. My heart missed a beat as the very word barrister conjured up visions of thousands of pounds in legal fees.

Two days later we were travelling north to meet this lady. We were pleasantly surprised, because she certainly did not fit the stereotype we were expecting. Christina was young, friendly, approachable and sympathetic and it was not long before I began to realise that we had a great deal in common. She was unconventional, astute and I knew she had the particular abilities needed for our case. We entered into a financial arrangement whereby we only had to pay a portion of her costs at that stage. The rest would be paid after a settlement, if that was achieved.

After a few months of contact between Christina and the Head Office of the bank we seemed, at last, to be making progress. The process of 'Discovery' (this is a legal process whereby we were given access to banking documents relating to our personal affairs and meetings with our Bank Manager) exposed glaring discrepancies between what was recorded and what had actually taken place, which the Head Office could not account for. Our old farm came onto the market again and Christina took advantage of the situation. She offered the bank a chance to compensate us for the injustice they had inflicted, by suggesting that they should help us return to the farm. A further meeting took place between Christina and a representative from the bank. We were asked, by the bank, to supply the estate agents' details about the farm for them to consider. Our hearts were in our mouths.

Whilst the legal battle accelerated, family life in the farmhouse took on a distressing turn. Up until this time we, as a family, had only experienced the positive side of man's relationship with unseen energies, with the exception of the small brush with negative energies in the vicinity of our own old farm. (Chapter Twenty) There we had come to understand that the energy passing through the farm was meeting a resistance in a nearby village. The energy line passed over ground that had witnessed black and evil events that had taken place there in past years. At one time this piece of land had been the site of a Warlock's abode, but, now had a modern bungalow built on it. I once stood on the point of these black vibrations and had felt very sick – wanting to run away from them as fast as I could. The block of negative energy that had been created by these black events was cleansed and released by an expert and the energies through our farm had begun to flow freely once again.

Shortly after moving into this new farm, it became obvious to me that I had, at some time in the past, lived on the site of the old farmhouse. I felt a familiarity with it, which was later to be confirmed by more than one of my many psychic friends. We were aware that the farm was located on an ancient preaching site marked by an Ash tree. In times past monks from the nearby abbey had preached to the local inhabitants under the Ash tree.

On the second day in this farmhouse, I stood on the upstairs landing, looking out the window. I was dressed in what felt like Quaker or Puritan dress. I felt lonely, cold and oppressed. I knew I lived in this home before and it had not been a happy situation for some reason. I had an overwhelming feeling that I really did not want to be here again.

As I have stated earlier, living on a powerful but positive site can be a very uplifting experience, and such energy can be used and projected in a very beneficial way. To find oneself actually living over a site of intense negativity is a very different situation. I now was beginning to realise that our home had extremely black and restless energies within, possibly as a result of past events. The effect it had upon us all was dramatic, distressing and very difficult to cope with and understand. However, there must be light within darkness and the result of the experiences that followed added to our understanding of the complexities of life and the many-faceted layers involved in living.

Out of respect for the privacy of various family members, I will not elaborate upon the effect the site had other than to say that daily living became increasingly difficult. In particular there were certain places in the farmhouse and outbuildings that were trigger points for trouble. When in the house alone, on several occasions, I heard the sound of a fist hammering on the heavy old wooden front door. The dogs in the house heard the sound as well and rushed with me to the door, barking excitedly. There was never anybody to be seen on the other side. At other times I would hear heavy footsteps on the staircase.

During the eighteen months at the farmhouse I found it very hard to maintain the will to keep going and had to dig very deeply into my own reserves. I had to hold on to the belief that life is a gift and try to reach an understanding of what this experience was all about. During that difficult period, one of our dogs fell backwards down the staircase in the middle of the night and broke its back and my beautiful horse that I had loved and ridden for some fifteen years, died of what appeared to be a heart attack, outside my bedroom window. It had felt all along that the site was baying for blood.

At a time of extreme desperation, during these experiences, I called to see two very good friends – Christopher and Anna. Anna was the author of a book I had helped her to self-publish. For many years, her husband, Christopher, had been an Anglican Vicar and both had worked in the realms of psychic rescue and healing. This had been the subject matter of Anna's book. It was Christopher who first brought some degree of peace back to the site. Some readers may find it unusual that an Anglican Vicar would be involved in such work but I already knew Christopher to be a knowledgeable and compassionate man whose reputation was well known.

I arrived at their West Dorset home in the middle of a winter afternoon. I had not seen either of them since moving to the farm in

Somerset and the first question Christopher wanted to ask was how I was feeling. He had a worried expression on his face and was not in the least surprised when I told him of our experiences at the farm. He told me that he knew, instinctively, when I first told him we were moving to the farm, that we were moving to a site of extreme negativity. He said he felt he could not tell me so at the time but hoped that we would be able to cope and possibly rise above the vibrations. Obviously it had not been possible to do so. That same afternoon he insisted both he and Anna would visit us that evening as he did not want us to spend another night in the farmhouse without help. It involved this elderly couple travelling a considerable distance across country on a winter's night and so I was very aware of how important they considered a visit to be.

I understood that help was going to involve the rescue and redirecting of the souls of people who had, at one time, lived on the site of the farm. For some reason or other they had not been able to release themselves from the site. They were left in limbo, a common phenomenon following sudden or violent death experiences and also relevant to souls of people unaware of their immortality. This very negative state of affairs meant that their vibrations still influenced the site and could affect our lives detrimentally. Such sites often evoke re-enactment and we were aware that our relationships were all under extreme strain.

Christopher's intention would be to make telepathic contact with these damaged souls and encourage them to leave their earthbound existence by moving them towards the light or higher realms. There they would gradually be able to move forward again. Such experience would bring enlightenment, healing and redirection to these lost souls, eventually leading to rebirth. Their past life experiences could then be drawn upon to shape future lives in a positive way.

Anna and Christopher arrived quite late in the evening. They had experienced trouble locating us because they drove into heavy fog around the vicinity of the farm and yet had not encountered fog anywhere else. It had been so dense they had almost given up hope of finding us. Christopher put water into a glass, blessed it and proceeded to move around the house splashing the water about. He came up against extreme negative energy blocks in certain parts of the farm-house. A major site was in the kitchen, by the doorway, and Brian and I were well aware that it had been a particularly bad area for trouble to erupt. However, we had not disclosed this to Christopher. We observed him – almost wrestling with an energy force whilst giving out blessings and prayers for the release of the damaged souls. Another area of trouble was the landing, where I had felt so much detail of a previous lifetime in the farmhouse. The worst place was outside in the great, big old stone barn. Nobody had felt happy in that barn and it had a horrible cold feeling about it and had been the trigger point for machinery breaking down, accidents and emotional outbursts between members of the family.

Christopher looked exhausted when they left around eleven o'clock that evening. We were eternally grateful to him for his help. Later I questioned Christopher about what had taken place at the farm to cause such a build up of negative energy. However he was not willing to give details of the events because he was concerned about the effect it might have. He said it would be better if we did not visualise those events as it would give power back to them. Far better that we understood that the necessary clearance of distressed souls had taken place and that we could now begin to live a more peaceful existence. He added that it would not be instantaneous and improve-ments would take several months, particularly as we had all been mentally damaged by our experiences and needed time to heal.

I still had no understanding of what my part had been in this unfolding mystery. I felt I might never do so, other than have faint recollections of a life as a Puritan girl in Somerset a few hundred years before. However, within a few months I was to gain a greater insight. It was the day of the funeral of Princess Diana. Brian and I were alone in the farm. We had been out riding our horses early in the morning as it was a beautiful day. We came back to watch the funeral on the television. We were sitting in the lounge, with the dogs at our sides. About fifteen minutes into the funeral proceedings I became aware of a very tall man standing outside the lounge window which faced a rear door of the farmhouse. I was seeing what I like to refer to, these days, as a 'yesterday's person'. His presence bought a shiver down my spine. I told Brian and expressed the fact that I did not wish to see this man's eyes because I had a great fear of them. The dogs also seemed transfixed, looking silently up at the window. The man was dressed in a black cloak with a huge brimmed black hat.

I tried to erase the presence of this man from my mind and get on with watching the funeral but he did not go away. After some thirty minutes I felt the room around me filling with white light. Brian and I were both aware of this light. It was not an unpleasant experience. Then I witnessed the plaster on the walls falling away and I could see the original bare stone of the farmhouse. Brian did not see this but continued to experience the light. I then saw the stone walls falling away and could clearly see that the farmhouse site was on a mound. Surrounding the mound, down on one knee, with muskets pointed at the site of the farmhouse, were twenty or thirty soldiers in black and white uniforms. They had buckles on their shoes, buckled sashes around their waists and were wearing small round helmets.

I could sense myself moving towards a big door to respond to a heavy fist hammering on it. I opened the door and looked into the cold dark eyes of the tall man in the black cloak, wearing the large brimmed black hat with a huge white plume feather in it. He handed me a rolled up piece of paper. It contained notification that we were, as a community, charged with hiding a fugitive who was on the run from what I assume were Royalists. I may have been experiencing a scene from the times of Cromwell. I knew we were innocent of the accusation and yet what followed appeared to be some kind of search of the farm and massacre of people and animals. Fortunately I was spared the details.

I felt I was experiencing a situation that required rescue from the trauma of its own history. I had seen Christopher, and others like him, work in the area and I knew what I had to do. I prayed, blessed and forgave those souls involved and implored them to move on to other brighter and higher realms of existence.

I returned to the reality of our lounge and the funeral of the

Princess of Wales on television. I felt extreme relief, almost joy, at what had transpired because I had gained a deep insight into the past events that had polluted the environment of that farm and I had played a small part in the clearance of those horrible vibrations. I had always admired and respected those who worked in the realms of psychic rescue though I had never had any desire to work in that area myself. However, spontaneously, having learned from observing others at the same work, I had reacted.

Brian had remained silent through these events, realising that I was in some kind of strange dream-like state and obviously dealing with something connected to the light in the room and man with the frightening eyes. When I told him what had happened he was relieved we seemed to have solved the mystery about just why it had been our fate to live at that farm. I felt, and so did Brian, that the time to leave had now arrived. We both very much wanted to move on. The site was now cleansed for others and we had earned a release from past memories.

Seven months later Brian and I moved further south in Dorset to a beautiful thatched cottage surrounded by a large rambling garden, a river, and a field for the horses to live in. Yet again we had found another wonderful home to rent whilst we continued to wade through the ongoing legal battle with our ex-bankers. I knew my work was finished at the farm and it was time for fresh horizons and for us all, as a family, to regain our independence. Paul's business had flourished at the farm despite all the negativity we had lived through. He was now in a position to move on and buy a farm of his own with Katherine.

It is interesting that the rescue of the damaged souls at the farm took place on that sad day of the funeral of Princess Diana. It seemed that the national emotion on that day was unified and loving, and maybe, it needed such emotion to trigger the event we had experienced. Perhaps the energy of love was so strong, across the nation, that the historical trauma at our site had become sufficiently focussed so that we could deal with it.

Just one week prior to moving to our new home, I called into a

local Somerset reference library, with my Daughter, to see if we could trace the history of the farm. We were told that most of the records relating to the area were away in Taunton, being re-compiled, so there was little information we could get at. Maybe that is just as well, because readers might think I had read the records first and then invented the tale – a not unreasonable suspicion in the present cultural climate. However, with my hand on my heart, I do say that is not so.

There was one small book in the library, taken from a locked glass cabinet by the librarian. She searched the index for the name of our farm and found that the site had been the location of secret Puritan meetings following the 'driving out' of a Puritan preacher from a local village. We also discovered that skeletons, in shallow graves, had been found on the hill at the entrance of the farm driveway when the new Turnpike Roads had been constructed. Incidentally that driveway entrance had, over the years, proved to be an accident black spot! The records for that village in Somerset, relating to the arrest, imprisonment and transportation of people involved in the Cromwellian uprisings have been lost for all time, although they still existed for other Somerset villages! One day, perhaps, we shall learn what actually happened.

I would add that several other, very psychically gifted, friends came to the farm to assist us during those distressing times. One particular elderly lady, who had worked at psychic rescue for many years, helped other souls on the site, who had become trapped in limbo between this reality and the next, probably attracted because of the negativity that had built up over the years. She found the souls actually queuing for her help at the site of the Ash tree. This same lady told me that my beautiful horse, who had died outside of my bedroom window, had died 'in service' to me, on that site. In a way I could believe her. The evening prior to his death, I had gone out into the field to talk and make a fuss of him. I had stayed with him for an hour, telling him how much I loved him and how he was 'worth his weight in gold' – by the morning he was gone – but he will never be forgotten and we took his cremated ashes and buried them in the garden of the thatched cottage we had moved on to.

It is well known that cleansing of damaged sites and the rescue of souls sometimes has to take place over a period of time, almost as if in waves. Such a comparison could be the allied war graves in Europe or the sites of the Concentration Camps. Here psychic mediums can return, year after year, and yet still find souls needing help to move onwards.

CHAPTER TWENTY SIX

Despite valiant efforts, involving many meeting with officials of the bank, Christina failed to obtain a settlement. On the one occasion the bank officials summoned Brian and myself and Christina to the Head Office, she advised us that they were either going to buy back our farm for us, or pay us a substantial amount of money by way of compensation, so sure was she that we were close to a result. Christina also advised us this would probably involve Brian and I having to sign a 'Gagging Order' – i.e. we would not be able to disclose publically what had happened. Christina was called into the room, ahead of us, and half an hour later came out ashen faced. At the eleventh hour, the bankers withdrew from all negotiations. Brian and I were devastated, and felt we had been 'baited'. Incensed and on Christina's advice we handed the files to the police and there followed months of protracted investigations, involving the Director of Public Prosecutions. Eventually we were advised that, although our complaint against the bank straddled both criminal and civil law, the case was more of a civil one. The ball was thrown back into our court to take civil action.

On the 31st Dec. 1997, whilst these investigations were proceeding, Brian and I decided to visit a recommended medium. We were on the verge of abandoning our four and a half year legal battle as we were so drained of energy and lacked the enthusiasm to continue. We felt ourselves floundering in a sea of words and trickery. The medium, with the interpretation of his guides, gave an accurate picture of our situation and then the spirit energy of my long-dead Father contacted us through him. His detailed description of himself and the illness that finished his life, left us in little doubt of the authenticity of this contact. My Father begged us both not to 'hang up the white flag'. He assured us that, if we had the strength to continue, we could achieve justice. He felt we would have to issue proceedings against the bank in order to achieve this.

We were greatly encouraged by this close contact with my dead Father. It was not the first time in recent years that he had managed to get critical advice through to us. (Chapter Fifteen) We agreed that we would give a last little piece of energy to the battle and put our faith in the wisdom of those who were trying to help us from the 'other side'. In March 1998 we were told by Christina that we were running out of legal time and that we would have to get a Writ issued in order not to have our dispute 'time barred' from court. This Writ would have to be served upon the Bank within four months of issue, taking us to July 1998. We had not been aware of the legal time scale and were heartened that the action we had now been forced to take had been predicted by my Father. At the beginning of June 1998 the bank were advised that a Writ had been issued and that it would be served shortly. We gave them yet another chance to return to settlement discussions and yet again they declined, referring to me as 'a loose cannon', the definition of this being: 'An unpredictable person or thing, liable to cause damage if not kept in check by others'. In hindsight I can see that this was a loaded statement, in view of all that transpired with the banking collapse later in 2010, resulting from their irresponsible lending activities. When I related our understanding of dubious Bank policies to colleagues in 1998, they were sceptical to say the least. What we were experiencing then was but the tip of the iceberg!

On 13th July 1998 I (and not Brian, for legal reasons), served the Writ on the Bank. I was now involved in a power struggle, which Christina told me had much more to do with 'brinkmanship'. They could, at any time, surrender and offer a settlement 'out of court' and I now waited expectantly for the one ingredient I needed to carry the case beyond the mere issuing of a Writ. That ingredient, I so desperately needed was Legal Aid. Without it I did not have the funds to enable me to take on a massive banking organisation with limitless resources. The bank, of course, knew this fact. I was very aware that Legal Aid was a scarce commodity and it was very much in the balance whether I would qualify. Apart from the tense legal situation, major psychic evidence was at stake as I had based the principles of my life on the relationship between these two states of reality, namely the in-body or physical and the non-physical or spiritual. The outcome was of enormous importance, not just because of the money involved, but because my trust in this relationship of realities, which had been building up during life, was now being put to the test. I knew there were those, in other realities, who wanted success for us, but I was also aware that the 'system' I was attempting to rock, was very powerful and that there would be people, with it, who were determined to silence me! If I was successful, many other, small, defenceless victims would take heart. Victims who had suffered unnecessarily and unjustly as the result of aggressive tactics employed during the recession, by bankers, who were more interested in lining their own pockets and looking after their shareholders than their customers.

Just a few days after the serving of the Writ, Christopher and Anna, who had helped us so much with the disturbed souls at the previous farm, came to see us in our new cottage home. Brian and I and the animals were very happy to be living in the cottage because if felt peaceful, warm and homely. In many ways it reminded us of our first beautiful cottage home, where this story began. However, we were only too well aware that we were not alone in our cottage. Once again there was evidence of 'Yesterday's People' and, in particular, I was aware of a lady who had once lived in the cottage, who had helped to look after children in the nearby estate house. She felt kindly towards me. Brian and I could also sense people dancing, in the oldest part of the cottage, to the music we often played.

A few days before moving in, I had visited the cottage and went from room to room placing a 'blessing of light'. The cottage was some four hundred years old and there was a considerable possibility that various souls still hung around it for a variety of reasons. I felt the need to talk with them. I sensed that they had not had very easy lives, all those years ago, for life would have been hard for workers on the country estate to which the cottage still belonged. I felt the need to tell them that life had been testing for Brian and me and that, in a way, we would be coming there to become strong again. I asked them to live in peace and harmony with us.

Christopher and Anna immediately felt the presences, including the lady I had sensed. However, Christopher also felt that many of those souls around us had suffered poor health as a result of hard work and damp living conditions. The cottage was surrounded by a river on three sides. Following the same procedure he used at the farm, he filled a glass of water and blessed it. Then moving from room to room he splashed the water about to bless the souls and encourage them to move towards the light of other realms. Unlike his work at the farm, the exercise felt much more peaceful and I was glad that we could help those souls and bring great peace to our cottage home.

As my reader may be well aware by now, I like to have evidence, that events I have experienced are true and not a figment of my imagination. Our experiences in the ancient farmhouse in Somerset

related to the English Civil War and were dramatic and frightening. Shortly after we moved away from that site and settled into our new cottage home, an old friend, who was a medium we had not seen for several years, turned up on our doorstep. Within a few minutes of being with us Roy began to describe a tall Cavalier standing by my side, who he said was a 'Yesterday's Person'. The Cavalier wanted to thank me for helping him move on. He said his name was Sir Galburth de Lise and that he had been married to a devoted wife and had Fathered their deformed child. He felt this event was the influence of Divine Justice in his later life. He perceived the Angel in the presence of the child, yet recognised the Devil in the physical appearance of him. He also said that John Lloyd, my Researcher and once Sir Henry Uvedale, had gone forward in another lifetime to be Sir Galburth de Lise. Roy sketched a picture of the Cavalier, and for sure he had the same frightening eyes that I had seen in that farm-house on the day the traumatic past events revealed themselves to Brian and me for healing.

For Brian and me it was a great relief to hear from the Cavalier. It allowed us to see some justification in the reason for our move to that particular site, upon which we had not been able to enjoy life.

As the years moved on our legal progress almost ground to a halt and my concerns regarding the power of the 'establishment' to protect itself were graphically illustrated. After serving the Writ, a solicitor had been appointed to carry the case onwards. This solicitor, on one occasion, wrote a letter to me containing the following alarming statement:

'One of my barristers is always at pains to point out to clients that judges are always formerly establishment barristers and if they are establishment barristers, they are the sort of barristers who have acted for Banks, insurance companies etc. in the past and therefore they naturally have some faith in the people that were formerly their clients. They are also the type of persons that play golf etc. with directors of Banks!'

I suspected that he was trying to tell me that, no matter how justified the case against my ex-Bankers might be, the chance of obtaining justice was very slim. Perhaps this is why the Bank knew it was quite safe, all those months before, to withdraw from settlement negotiations. They knew the 'establishment' would close ranks on me and the Bank would be protected from successful prosecution. After all I was a 'loose cannon'!

Now I was becoming aware that there was a distinct possibility that I would gain neither a moral nor a financial victory – a very hard lesson for a citizen to learn. In a desperate attempt to adopt a philosophical view and to ease my frustration, I allowed myself to sense the parallel with my upbringing in the establishment religion and the battle to liberate myself from that. Once again I was up against the establishment, this time in the legal area, and it was evident that this was going to prove a little harder to reconcile. Perhaps it was more important that I had done my very best to protest to 'the system' about systematic violation. In any event the anti-establishment ripples I shall continue to send out, by including the legal battle as part of this book, will draw attention to such injustices and, perhaps, encourage others to protest. Constraints within our religious and social structures, that deny personal freedom and individuality, need to be challenged.

For five years Brian and I had poured a great deal of energy into our search for justice. Alongside that, life had been charged with powerful events and situations. We can only deduce that we have drawn these circumstances to ourselves in order to grow in under-standing and we realise, as a result of our experiences, that we are much stronger and more philosophical. We may have lacked financial security, but we had one another, we were well and living in a beautiful home in a wonderful part of the country, surrounded by family, animals and friends. We looked at a rapidly changing and unstable world around us and anticipated that is was going to be difficult for many people to adjust to the chaos of transition as the world moved into the Aquarian era.

Our legal case against the Bank continued. We took a step forward and then it seemed several steps backwards. It became obvious, as the months passed, that our solicitor was reluctant to work at our case. Other clients of the solicitor, with litigation in progress against Banks, experienced the same problem. A new solicitor had to be appointed and yet again a terrible lethargy in moving the case forward became evident. During this frustrating period Brian and I came into contact with others litigating against Banks and all were experiencing 'stone walling' by the investigating police authorities and reluctant solicitors. Eventually our solicitor told us he thought it not worth continuing the litigation and told us to take the story to the newspapers. We could not believe what we were hearing. This solicitor knew, only too well, that something very wrong had transpired and yet legally he felt inept to expose it.

Our M.P. wrote, on our behalf, to the Director of Public Prosecutions requesting him to ask the police to re-investigate. Yet again a totally negative response was received. It was now apparent to us that the 'system' was closing in on our case and those of many others. The Banking system is all-powerful and its tentacles of influence are far reaching.

Throughout the years of this titanic legal struggle Brian and I have asked ourselves whether or not we were dealing with another karmic issue which had yet to authenticate itself. The intimidating use of power and influence had been inflicted on us by a particular person within the Bank and with whom we had enjoyed a friendly and trusting relationship for many years. It was this person's denial of his actions that had caused the protracted litigation. From written evidence we accessed during the 'Discovery' period, it was very obvious that power had been misused and the Bank knew this. The denial of the perpetrator, however, allowed the Bank to relinquish their responsibility. As long as that denial existed, the case could not be resolved.

As our legal case began to collapse I could not help but feel there had to be a deeper reason for this situation. I decided to 'test the water'. I placed the name of the particular individual concerned, who had refused to own up to his actions, in a sealed envelope and gave it to my good friend Mary the medium who had been Mother to Brian and me some four hundred years prior. (Chapter Twenty Three) Mary

I knew had a considerable ability at psychometry, this being the ability to read the energy contained in an object or, in my case, the name of a person written and placed inside a sealed envelope. Such psychic investigation was something she had been asked to do, time and time again, in respect of missing people, to assess integrity or to judge compatibility of people. I was not all together surprised to learn from Mary that I had a karmic link to the person named in the envelope. She told me that several hundreds of years ago I had betrayed this man in connection with smuggling activities in Cornwall. This time he was betraying me. Mary gave us a lot of details about the individual. This information contained graphic evidence, in respect of details, that convinced us that Mary had 'tuned in' accurately, as we already knew quite a lot about the person.

Why had it taken so long for the penny to drop? Possibly because there had been other frustrated energies that needed to be exorcised from our souls throughout the duration of the litigation; those energies, relating to other lives and experiences, that I have already mentioned in previous chapters.

For sure we know that life, today, is a multi-levelled experience. We are obviously trying to balance and wipe clean the karmic slate. Maybe that is the most important thing we can do this time around. We now believe 'success' in life has more to do with spiritual perception and growth rather than physical and material achievement. In the material world it is a brave philosophy to adopt and, materially, a bitter pill to swallow. As the years have passed, my evaluation of what is valuable, and more importantly what is not, has undergone a massive transformation. Could this be the lesson for us all in this life? The words from the Lord's Prayer come to mind: 'And forgive us our trespasses, as we forgive them that trespass against us'. I like to think, that even in the early stages of litigation, Brian and I had already come to the feeling that we had forgiven the individual who would not own up to the truth of the situation. We felt he was as much a victim of brutal Banking recession policies as we were, from comments he had made to us about the way Banks treat their staff. He had only carried out Head Office recession directives. However, at this stage, we can only feel extreme contempt for the organisation itself for turning a blind eye to our plight. That is an immoral act of inhumanity. But, perhaps individuals have to change spiritually speaking, before there can be any hope for the establishment!

As a result of our experiences we understand that we must embrace change without fear. We are all on the planet to grow in understanding. One day we will have served our apprenticeships and, after many incarnations, will be ready to return to our blissful origins in other worlds. Hopefully, we will have left behind a new world that will have embraced a holistic mantle. Brian and I understand that what has taken place in previous lives has influenced us this time around and our handling of these experiences will map our future lives. At this time, despite all the uncertainties, we felt positive. The future felt expansive. What next?

PART THREE
TRANSFORMATION

The Book of Life – by Michael Berman

On the top of sacred mountain
From the rock foundations rises crystal palace
And in the womblike chamber that lies within its centre
On a crystal dais I found the Book of Life

I turned the pages to find they stopped at the present
For it was up to me to fill in what comes next
Then to set out with my newfound sense of purpose
And to dance those pages awake

Then I joined the column descending the mountain
Programmed and intent on my task
And passed the column climbing to the summit
To write their futures in the book

Whenever I lose my way, I'll see the pages before me
To guide me back on to my path
And each time I'm blessed with a new dream
I'll return there to add it to my list.

CHAPTER TWENTY SEVEN

Today is now Wed. 16th August 2006 and I remember that this is how my writing began eighteen years ago. As was then, I again feel the need to begin to write because I know something is going to happen in my life and I am aware of the need to record events to date, because they are all relevant to what about is to happen. I now respect my intuition a little more these days.

Sometimes it is just a case of getting on with life on a daily basis with all its joys, sorrows and tribulations. On a day to day basis I know it is important to just live and deal with what presents. When I completed my first book 'The Return', many years ago now, I thought that was it and that I couldn't possibly expect anything else of such 'other world' magnitude to ever happen again. In hindsight I can see it was but an initiation into a journey that is ongoing and challenging. However, knowledge gained from past experience and new tools are always awaiting us in the wings of life. An army of beings, from the other worlds, are there watching and hoping that we can remember to ask for their help, for without that invitation we have to find our own way, as they cannot interfere. Our life is our journey to live at our own pace and choice. We all come with a mission, I understand and it is our choice as to whether we embrace and search it out or live life as a leaf in the breeze. There is no right or wrong way, just choice. Life can be multi-dimensional if we choose. Some parts of my life have needed to be very worldly based. It is my awareness of these earthly experiences that is measured internally by some deep connection that tells me whether something needs to change to bring me closer into line with what I should be doing. Possibly I could say 'bringing heaven' whatever that may be to any of us, 'a little more into sync with earth'.

Several years have now passed and much water has passed under the bridge in those years. For me they have been the most meaningful of the last eighteen years, in so much, as allowing me to become more comfortable about my unworldly experiences. The last few years have seen the culmination of all that the past experiences had been building up to. The world is changing. All that we were told about psychically, all those years ago, is coming to pass and I am a part of something exciting, wonderful and at times daunting.

So I will begin, once again, to relate what has transpired during the last few years to bring us to this point, doubtless during this process, further unexpected happenings will unfold ready for me to document.

Within days of writing 'what next', at the end of Chapter Twenty Six, the owner of that beautiful cottage, where we had felt so at home, served notice on us. He wanted to convert the cottage into holiday accommodation. We felt devastated because we really did not want to leave. We had felt so at home in the cottage and its environment. However, life was about to move us on again.

The estate on which the cottage was situated had a well-known ancient manor house, Athelhampton House, near Dorchester in Dorset, dating back to the times of Henry VII. It was open to the public and one of the charms of the property were the stories of the various ghostly appearances. Just prior to our leaving, a television crew had been invited into the manor house, by the owner, in an attempt to film ghostly happenings. The intrusion had the effect of upsetting the 'Yesterday's People.' These souls needed to be seen and helped on their way, having become trapped in a state of limbo. They had just forgotten how to leave the earth life behind, as I have mentioned before in this book; they had no idea or memory, in their last life upon earth, that they were eternal beings and could move on to other worlds, with a choice to either return again for an earthly life or to move on elsewhere.

Disturbing phenomena had involved a Grand Piano playing without a pianist and an ancient baby cradle had been rocking unaided, which the young and sensitive wife of the owner had found disturbing and frightening. Knowing of my familiarity with such happenings, she called me in to try and settle the activity.

Late on a winter's evening I walked the passageways and corridors of the ancient house with her and communed with the spirits of 'Yesterday's People' silently. I did my best to convey to them the wisdom of moving on. I also tried to explain to them that the promotion of their existence, in this historic house, had drawn the public in. The monies earned from this public exposure helped to finance the maintenance of the beautiful old house, without which it probably would not have survived in such a beautiful condition.

Feedback from the young lady of the manor over the next few weeks showed that an understanding had been accepted by the 'Yesterday's People' and phenomena had ceased. As, however, with all ancient houses and sites, there are always many layers of psychic imprint, that will come to the surface to seek liberation, just like peeling away layers of an onion. Maybe that was one of the reasons Brian and I were being forced to move on yet again. More work to be done elsewhere and completion on the site where we had been living happily for some four years.

Within a few weeks of being asked to leave, we found an idyllic cottage, set on a valley floor, with beautiful rolling hills surrounding. It was the site of an ancient Celtic settlement with a bridleway passing our front door. Only a few miles from the cottage we were leaving, it meant not too much disruption to our working lives. Brian was still working with our son in the manufacturing forge and I had been working locally, running two large complementary therapy associations, since the collapse of our Banking litigation. This work was arduous and repetitive, but it earned us some much needed funds and the great bonus was that my working environment, in a complementary therapy clinic, put me into contact with some very interesting people. New horizons began to open up for me and were very refreshing after the frustrations of the last few years. As well as running the associations, I returned to college to study hypnotherapy so that I could use my personal experience and knowledge of past lives, to help others access theirs. Invitations to travel and speak with audiences, following the publication of my original book, resulted in many of my readers making contact with me and asking for help unravelling their own multi-life memories.

Resulting from a new friendship forged whilst working in the complementary therapy clinic, I found myself, one weekend, visiting a Psychotherapy and Counselling school in Bournemouth. My decision to go was based on a couple of hours spent each week on a massage course. The new friend and partner I worked with, came to the session with such a feeling of stillness about her that I asked her what her work was or where she had been all day. Her response was that she was training to be a Psychospiritual Counsellor and Wednesday was her day of training. On expressing my desire to be able to feel that peaceful, she asked me if I would be interested in the training; however, when she told me it would take three years to gain a Higher National Diploma, I ruled the idea out as too time consuming in view of my financial need to earn my keep. A few weeks later she gave me the news that the Head of the School was going to leave the country within a couple of years to live in Canada and that he had decided to take one final intake into the school for an eighteen month intensive course. As this was to be the final training, I decided I needed at least to look into the possibility of enrolling, although I had very little idea of what the training would entail and why I felt such an interest in getting there. The next step was an introduction weekend.

Several floors above the busy shops in the centre of Bournemouth was The Sacred Space Institute of Counselling and Psychotherapy. As I walked through the doorway of the Institute I was greeted by clouds of smoke from burning white sage, an array of colour, regalia and sound hit me as I entered another world. Standing in front of me was John-Luke Edwards, a slight but powerfully presented man, with charisma just pouring off of his being. I was hooked at that moment. The day was interesting, but it was not the content of the day that hooked me so much as the space itself. I just knew I had to get there and so returned home and applied for a place on this last course to be held at the Institute. Little did I know that I was about to embark upon the journey of a lifetime. Nor did I have any idea of the academic input that would be required of me.

The next eighteen months felt like being 'out of time'. Every hour spent in the training was, in the early stages, painful and yet expansive, as the group of students began to share themselves emotionally, unravelling their psyches and re-synthesising them. We were an extremely mixed group of individuals of varying ages and many of us had experienced challenging and interesting life journeys. Gradually I explored all the schools of psychological thought including, in particular, Transpersonal Psychology and Psychosynthesis and I began to underpin all my own psychic and spiritual experiences with sound psychology. I came to realise, more than ever before, that I had been academically, socially, culturally and educationally denied many truths about my potential in this lifetime. On embarking upon the training, it had occurred to me that what I was about to learn could possibly cast a powerful doubt upon my 'other worldly' experiences to date. But that was not to be the case.

The psychology theories of Roberto Assagioli, who was an Italian Psychiatrist (1910 – 1974), hit the very core of my inner knowing. I began to delve deeply into myself, gaining insight into how I operated emotionally, from a mental and spiritual perspective to regain the choice I was born with, to become the person I really wanted to be.

My aim had been to find the still place that I had recognised in my partner on the massage course, but I found more than peace; I found my true self, buried under a multitude of defence mechanisms and fragmented parts. My reward, as a result of the time spent in training and research and many hours of personal therapy to help me re-evaluate my experience, was that I totally came alive and recognised the potential power at my finger tips to direct my life and enjoy it. I had embarked upon the training merely for the personal journey, However, inspired by my experience, I found myself moved to share it with others, and so began my new life as a Psychospiritual Counsellor.

Psychosynthesis recognises the artistic, altruistic, spiritual and heroic potentials of humanity. So the counselling process honours the whole core of the person, which includes the spiritual presence or higher self. The Psychosynthesis approach to counselling takes the view that each of us has a purpose in life and that we have challenges and obstacles to meet in order to recognise and fulfil that purpose.

We are not, in fact, one person, but various personalities and sub-personalities struggling continuously with each other; impulses, desires, principles and aspirations are often in conflict. The task of the Counsellor is to hold the sacred space that allows the client to bring clarity into this confusion.

We find that when the various elements of our being are in conflict, our energy becomes blocked, and this causes pain. However, each time that a synthesis of two or more parts of our personality occurs, energy is freed and we experience a sense of profound well-being – our spirit becomes free. This tendency towards synthesis is inherent within us all and once people understand themselves better they have much greater clarity, plus the power and freedom to make their own choices and exercise their own will.

Psychosynthesis, rather than being an artificial imposition of techniques, simply unblocks and stimulates a process that is more closely allied to us than any other – the growth of a whole being.

The role of the therapist is to support each person in exploring their presenting problems, at the same time reflecting back to them a sense of their whole being, including the mental, emotional, physical and spiritual aspects of self.

Psychosynthesis offers valuable techniques to support personal growth and find the doorways to each individual's potential, in the context of our complex and increasingly fragile world. The approach is creative and can involve the use of art work, journaling, visualisation, meditation and many other inventive avenues of personal discovery.

Within the first few weeks of beginning my training, I had also gone out in search of a therapy room to rent in order to practice my new found skills of hypnotherapy. I eventually arrived at a building on a local industrial estate, where rooms were being advertised for rent. I found myself in front of a large white building, which in itself looked attractive and quite old. The rooms to let were on the second floor. Deciding to go ahead and at least take I look, I was amazed as I walked into a beautifully presented environment, with therapy rooms, and a main teaching area, kitchen and toilets and shower. Even more so when the owner, who had been running the space as a yoga studio, told me that he was looking for somebody to take over the whole building because he could not make it pay. It all felt just too good to be ignored and I asked the owner to give me a couple of days to think it over.

My first thought was to find somebody to share the undertaking with me and share the expense of paying the rent and rates. The Chairman of both of the complementary therapy associations I had been running, who was himself a therapist, felt to me to be the first person to proposition, because I recognised a connection to him, dare I say it from a past life! He took the bait and we were in business within one month and from day one found enough therapists and tutors to rent space from us to cover the rent. And so came into being Body Mind Spirit in Dorset, a Complementary Therapy and Teaching Centre that now gave me a beautiful environment in which to work.

At the conclusion of my training at The Sacred Space Institute of Psychotherapy and Counselling and following its closure and the departure from this country of my charismatic tutor, two other students and I took the essence of the training and opened up a similar training for counsellors at Body Mind Spirit. During the first year of the school's development, I team-taught with my two colleagues and we all went back to college to study for our teaching qualifications at the same time as we taught our students.

CHAPTER TWENTY EIGHT

Brian and I now had two new horses. Our dear old friends, who had lived with us for the past twenty years, had left this world. To part with a horse, with which you have shared a beautiful relationship for years, can be devastating. Now many years on, I still miss their unique personalities. However, we have to move on and one of the new arrivals was Merlin – a magnificent, confident gypsy driving horse who gave us many hours of pleasure, driving us around the lanes of Dorset and Somerset. The other was an Irish Piebald Cob, very young, having lived just three very insecure years. He had not been badly treated but, in his very short life to date, he had had to do more than was really comfortable for a young horse. He presented himself as very needy and thrived on attention and love. Brian and I had spent many wonderful hours riding and living with our previous three horses, but these two young ones had now come to take us to the next stage of understanding, the bond between horse and human and the potential in that bond.

The relationship began to unfold whilst we were living at the cottage in the ancient Celtic valley towards the end of my training. Danny-Boy, the little Irish Piebald began to show signs of weakness in his legs. He looked sturdily built, with strong-looking legs, but he definitely had to struggle when it came to walking up hills. Strangely, at the same time, I began to have trouble with my legs. They ached day and night, my knees were swollen and stiff and I could only stand for a few minutes before I lost all power in them

At that stage my greater concern was for Danny-Boy; he was young and he should have been fit and strong. I had heard, via some therapy colleagues, of a lady who worked as an Energy Therapist both for humans and animals, and especially horses, to whom she was able to tune in as a 'horse whisperer'. So I gave her a call about Danny-Boy. Pam asked me to send her a cutting of Danny-Boy's mane so she could dowse over it to find what was causing him his problem. Within a couple of days of receiving the cutting she called and said she needed to come and work with him as he had some emotional conflicts that were affecting his physical body.

Danny-Boy was standing in his Paddock with Merlin as Pam arrived. I put a halter on him and brought him over to meet Pam, who began to run over his body with a pendulum reading his energy system. She also began to relate the story of his experiences from birth until his present age of five years, some of which I was aware of, via his previous owner, from whom I had bought him aged three. The story she told was one of sadness, loss and fear, that no young horse should ever have had to endure, yet many do. Pam learned that he had been suddenly taken away from the field in which he lived with his Mother and another friend horse, transported via lorry and ship to England and sold to a dealer, who then went on to sell him to a young girl. This young girl was the person I had bought him from and although she had treated him very lovingly, during the time she owned him, she had sent him away to be broken to harness when he was just eighteen months old. Danny-Boy told Pam how scared, tired and hungry he had been during this training. His previous owner had told me about his trip away to harness training and so I knew Pam was truly interpreting the horse. As he told me all this I was holding onto his mane and felt intense sadness coursing through my body and down through my feet into the ground. Tears poured from my eyes and I felt like I was a conductor, flushing his anguish into the earth. Pam continued to work on his energy centres, using her pendulum to help open up the closed meridians and help the flow of chi around his body. She told me that he carried so much grief in his heart meridian, it was causing him breathing difficulties and oxygen was not feeding into his blood stream correctly and servicing his young legs properly; this explained his exhaustion when walking up hills.

Pam left me with some homoeopathic remedies for Danny-Boy, to help his healing further and I have to say the energy improvement for Danny-Boy was instantaneous. What took much longer to correct was helping him to gain inner confidence and autonomy, but I did not want to rush the process. I had all the time in the world and this was my first experience of working with a young and damaged horse. I had a lot to learn and he was going to teach me. The blessing for Danny-Boy was that he was now sharing his life with a beautiful, wise and courageous horse – Merlin.

Merlin's origins were a very different story. He had been bred by a Gypsy with a reputation for breeding and raising magnificent driving horses, and Merlin was certainly that, when I bought him at the tender age of five. Nothing ever worries Merlin. He presents as a deep horse and it has always felt as though his wisdom went way beyond this lifetime. These two horses and their diverse characters were to have a profound effect on our lives for the next few years and the experience led us into a way of working together in a very unusual therapeutic partnership. In hindsight, it felt as though a powerful synchronicity existed between us, Danny-Boy's physical condition and mine, that culminated in my learning about another level of horse human interaction – Equine Assisted Therapy; I write here about the deep relationship that binds horse to human. When Danny-Boy was in his uncomfortable emotional state that I described, I was also having problems with my mobility, especially in my legs. Pam, energy therapist, dowsed for my underlying problem and found I had huge mineral and vitamin deficiencies that were caused by Candida in my gut. This seemingly quite simple diagnosis proved correct, despite the fact that the medical profession could not find out what wrong with me. I had been sent for hydro-therapy to ease my sore joints and lack of mobility, whilst a series of blood tests showed nothing significant, and professional suggestions were made that my problems were psychosomatic! It took four months of concentrated intake of products to cleanse the Candida from my gut, and an intake of mineral and vitamin supplements to get the power back into my legs. When I returned to the hospital to be examined for consideration for cartilage surgery, the Specialist could not believe my improvement. When I explained how I had returned to mobility, he was shocked, but not surprised. He said we can often look to more serious possibilities when looking into symptoms and in so doing overlook the very simple but obvious. Conventional medicine tends towards symptoms and not the cause, and this is where complementary medicine has so much depth and potential to offer. The whole person is considered before treatment begins.

During the time of my loss of mobility, I could not ride or drive Danny-Boy or Merlin and so spent a lot of time just being with them in their fields. Gradually I could see that my horses were able to pick up or intuit in some way what was going on emotionally for me – it was uncanny – I was given 'food for thought'. When I was feeling present and 'in the moment' my horses would draw in close to me and invite me to be a part of the resting herd. When my thoughts took me into the past or the future, the horses would move out of my space. If I owned my emotions in the moment and didn't try to disguise them, the horses would draw in close again, giving me the feeling that they were there supporting me. If I tried to mask sadness or anger from them, they would move away – the incongruence in my subtle body language and energy obviously seemed to make them feel uncomfortable.

These experiences moved me to seek out deeper knowledge of horses and their healing powers by researching in books and there I found masses of anecdotal evidence to support my growing understanding of their depth of perception. I began to realise, from my perspective as a Transpersonal Counsellor, that I could invite my horses to work alongside me with clients in their therapy process. They provided, as it were, a magnificent living and honest mirror. They became the perfect intuitive and creative therapeutic partners.

It was this experience that led me to search of a way to train in this model of therapy and, via a string of interesting synchronicities, I was then given the opportunity to do so with an organisation that originates from the USA – The Equine Assisted Growth and Learning Association – EAGALA www.eagala.org. This organisation now has a European training facility – www.eagala.org.uk. For me it felt as if I had been waiting all my life for this experience.

Equine Assisted Psychotherapy and Learning engages the ability of the horse to mirror unspoken human behaviour and emotions. The therapy, often worked in a therapeutic triad, of client, therapist and horse expert, using these mirroring abilities of the horse, is considered to be short-term and solution-based, allowing the client to regain their faculty of personal choice over their reactions within relationship with themselves and others.

What is it about horses that makes them so capable of this work and produce results so swiftly? For me the answer is found in their high sensitivity. Horses have to live very much in the moment for their daily survival – they have a powerful fight or flight survival mechanism and they are totally honest. Their senses are finely tuned to their environment and other herd members and they can pick up human thoughts and emotions and interpret body language and reflect it back to us for us to see. They allow us to see our patterns of relating and give us the opportunity to experiment with changing those ones that do not serve us well.

For me, horses are telepathic; you cannot lie to a horse and so, ultimately, you cannot continue to lie to yourself. Horses can help us to become authentic, remembering who we really are beyond our masks. To me they are the essence of Psychosynthesis.

My horses are now happier and more bonded as a herd than I have ever known before – it is as though I have allowed them to become whole and live to their full potential. That is the gift they offer to us as well! I need to add that two other horses eventually joined Merlin and Danny-Boy. Otto a thoroughbred horse who came all the way from Portugal to live with us and Blue, an aging small Highland Pony, who was looking for a good home to live out his later years. I need to write a little more, in general terms, about the upsurge in the use of horses worldwide in Equine Assisted Therapy in recent years. Over time I have seen examples of horses being abused for this purpose, possibly not intentionally by those who set out to work humans with horses, but through lack of understanding, on the part of the facilitators and trainers; also, of the high sensitivity of horses. They deserve our utmost respect, for horses are in touch with profound abilities that we humans, in most cases, have long forgotten are still available to us. It is these dormant abilities that horses seek to put us in touch with again and this is their gift to humanity, especially in a time when many speak about feeling totally at a loss about the purpose of their lives. People speak of feeling as if something is missing and the search for this missing inner peace leads to an external search for meaning. Dangerous diversions then have an opportunity to take a grip by way of addictions. The gift the horse offers is to help us to be put in touch with our authentic selves, so that we learn to relate to our true selves and not to the myriad of false selves we have adopted to survive our challenging lives. Many people today live very sterile, material lives, in urban environments where contact with the natural world is extremely limited. It is by turning back to the natural world that we can learn to live within the same energetic flow, to get back in touch with and trust our intuition, to feel our energetic responses within and make the right choices and responses in our relationships with ourselves and others.

During the course of our developing working relationship with horses, we moved home yet again. We remained at the cottage in our Celtic valley for only a short while during which I completed my counselling training and just long enough to be close to my Mother as she came to the end of her life at ninety-three. We then moved up into Somerset, to the farm where our son, Paul and his partner Kathy had been living since leaving the rented farm that we had shared with them, and where we experienced all the phenomena connected to the English Civil War. Brian had spent many years travelling to this farm on a daily basis to help with the running of the furniture manufacturing business. During that time, between manufacturing, Brian and Paul had managed to convert an old barn into a second home on the farm and it was to that property we next moved. At this farm, Brian and I began to work together as a therapy team with our four horses. Brian became my horse expert as there was nobody else who could read their body language better than him. The four horses soon became a tightly bonded herd, moving into therapy work as if they, too, had been waiting all their lives to be asked!

During our time living in that ancient valley, Brian and I had constantly been aware of a wild herd of 'Yesterday's Celtic Horses'. We often walked the valley floor in the moonlight with our dogs and would both be aware of a sensation of stampeding horses coming from behind us, and would stand still whilst the horses made their way around us. Sometimes when we were out riding along the valley, our horses would suddenly sense the approach of this huge energy and we would have to restrain them from wanting to 'run with the herd'.

When our time came to leave the cottage, we both felt sad to be leaving the etheric Celtic herd and so decided to invite them to move with us, to Somerset, to reside in the long and beautiful valley that the farm sat on the side of. This valley had been the site of a huge, ancient Medieval village. I felt I would be able to invite this 'Yesterday's Herd' to work with us on a higher level of contact in Equine Therapy. Brian and I never told anybody about this herd of horses. Five years after moving to the farm in Somerset, we met up with a very intuitive young lady who used to come and care for our animals when we went away on holiday. One day she just turned round to us and asked if we were aware that there was an etheric herd of Celtic Horses running on the valley floor below the farm. This kind of confirmation is always so gratefully received; as my readers will know, I like to be sure that what I see, feel and know, shows itself to others. We all need confirmation from time to time that we are not alone in our perceptions. It is our benchmark of authenticity.

CHAPTER TWENTY NINE

Our horses had brought us yet another great opportunity during 2007. Danny-Boy's arrival and emotional needs had caused us, those few years back, to look at alternative ways of training horses and we became very comfortable with natural horsemanship methods. Although considered a new approach, Natural Horsemanship is in fact ancient and goes back to the time when man was dependent upon horses for survival, so that the need for a good authentic relationship with them was imperative. When I speak of Natural Horsemanship I am talking about a method of being and working with horses that is extremely relational. Rather than training by domination, which has been and is still used to a great extent throughout the world, Natural Horsemanship involves inviting a horse to train energetically, responding to the trainer or riders body language. This is much the same way in which Equine Assisted Therapy works. A horse, because of its innate sensitivity, is able to pick up on a human's intent, emotionality and body language. This is how horses relate to each other within a herd. They have a huge social sensual awareness. Each herd member is able to pick up on what is going on for the other horses. They sense each other's flight or fight mechanism and so know when it is safe to relax and graze and when it is the time to move on. It is said that a horse can sense, when in the wild, if a lion several miles distant has eaten. If the lion is not searching for food then it is safe to graze. Once again I have to reiterate, this is the ability that the horses attempt to remind us that we ourselves have, if only we can quieten our minds and begin to listen again. After all, our own ancestors were once hunter-gatherers and they had to rely on their own flight or fight mechanism to survive.

Natural Horsemanship Training often makes use of circular training pens. These pens, made usually from metal, seem to originate from the USA, as do many modern Natural Horsemanship techniques. The old cowboys certainly knew how to relate to their horses. However, that is not to say all of them did. Many degrading and cruel methods of horse training were and are still used world-wide, as I have already mentioned. Natural Horsemanship training affords the horse its dignity. In order to work relationally and authentically, the trainer/owner has to become more horse-like. What is so pleasing to see is that Natural Horsemanship is on the increase worldwide, thanks to the likes of Monty Roberts and Pat Parelli and many, many other talented horsemen and women. We had need of such a circular pen to begin to work with Danny-Boy and help him gain his confidence again, and so, as we had a manufacturing forge, designing and producing one was a simple matter.

What a gift the evolvement of making circular training pens was to became for Brian and me. When other horse owners saw our pen at a demonstration at a local Equestrian College, they wanted one and so we went into production and set up our own training pen manufacturing business, operating via the fast growing retail medium of the internet. Our pens began to go out to horse owners all over the UK and eventually into Europe. For years Brian and I had wished we could invent something to make that others would want to use and buy, but more importantly, something we would enjoy making and being involved with. Although most pens went out to people via a carrier, the more local ones Brian and I delivered ourselves. We and our small dogs got a day out and we met up with many horse owners who themselves were turning to Natural Horsemanship methods. It felt as if the world of horse owners were waking up to a kinder way of working in relationship with their horses as opposed to training by domination. Creating one's own reality by thought projection and visualisation is a very interesting and hot topic these days in alternative and personal development fields and countless self-help books are available explaining techniques that can be adopted to help improve life prospects and make personal dreams come true. We had worked upon a desire to invent a product that we would enjoy selling. We had no idea what it would be. Our love of working with horses brought our dream into reality. So it works!!

However, I hasten to add that Natural Horsemanship is not a soft option of training. It requires focus and self-awareness on the part of the trainer as well as knowledge on how to relate authentically to the horse. Horses need good leaders they can trust, to work in relationship with. In fact, as I had already learnt, horses are wonderful teachers because they have to be authentic themselves in order to survive and this is why they are such great therapists to humans. It is my opinion, and I know the opinion of others who work in Equine Assisted Psychotherapy, that horses trained by Natural Horsemanship techniques, possibly make better therapy horses than those who have been desensitised into conforming to the wishes of their trainers. Natural Horsemanship is all about the use of energy, both through the mental intent and the use of good body language to convey what is being asked of the horse. Body language and social sensual awareness is how horses relate to each other. If owners have trouble relating to their horses, and blame the horse when the relationship does not work out and put it up for sale, they should perhaps look to themselves first to see if the problem lies in their own way of relating!

Horses that have had a troubled or deprived background can be retrained and given new opportunities to be themselves again. These horses often prove to be the most effective therapy horses in the long term and offer great insights to humans who themselves are battle-scarred by their own experiences.

To elaborate a little more about authentic horse-human relation-ship and the evidence of such, I would just like to add that I am not a brave horse rider. I was not involved with horses in childhood and so my first relationship with them began when our children were still quite young and I was in my twenties. I was very lucky that the horses that came into our lives then were happy and well-adjusted. Nobody, it would appear, had harmed them in any way and they had a great trust of humans. The horses were a very important part of our family, as were all our other animals. We were lucky to be able to have them living next to our home and so they were an integral part of everyday life and very important members of our family clan. I was always totally honest in my approach to them. If I went to ride one of them and felt, for some reason, a bit nervous on that day, I would think and say to my horse that I felt so and ask him/her to look after me and be aware I did not feel confident. Remarkably they always did just that. Or is it just remarkable? How many people have been told that when going to ride a horse, leave your emotions at the field gate? Here is the great mistake. We cannot disguise our emotions as humans and so the horses, in fact all animals, pick up on them and react accordingly. Horses reflect what is going on inside us. They can see beneath our masks and react accordingly and that is the gift they bring us, reflecting our true selves back to us in a way that no human therapist can. When we are authentic and living in the moment they want to be with us. When we leave our centre point and are not present, they sense this and do not feel safe and will move away. If a rider works a horse by using domination and restrictive riding tools, eventually such incongruence can lead to disaster and danger for both horse and rider. For this very reason, a considerable amount of equine therapy works well with the horses being at liberty, free to move away if they feel uncomfortable. I like to work my clients out on the open fields, with the herd together and free to either be with the client or not. This choice of the horse to be with the client or not is the authenticity mirror.

CHAPTER THIRTY

In March 2009 disaster struck. Brian became seriously ill and we were about to embark upon yet another challenge of a lifetime. At first we had no idea what was making him so unwell. He saw a doctor who ran a few inconclusive tests and then put him on a long waiting list to see a hospital Specialist. He was losing weight rapidly, felt cold all the time and was generally very unwell and could not work. We told the doctor we suspected Brian's condition could be related to his work in tbe forge, where many hazardous fumes and chemicals were present. We waited four months for the Specialist appointment, which we had requested should be urgent, during which time Brian's health deteriorated at an alarming rate and I had to stop working to look after him. In desperation we sought the help of a medical dowser called Uta Rogers, who worked as a Vibropath, (i.e. a Homoeopath using vibrational remedies) Uta immediately told Brian he had polyester resin inside him. It had burnt his respiratory tract, caused bleeding behind his eyes, affected his hearing and cognition and was wreaking havoc in his digestive system. He was losing weight rapidly and was virtually unable to eat anything and keep it inside of him and he was losing his balance.

I need to add here that Uta reaches her diagnostic conclusions by the use of Medical Dowsing. Many such therapists rely on this wonderful innate human ability to dowse. Brian himself had shown remarkable dowsing abilities in more recent years in finding lost animals and items, often in foreign countries. This is what Uta has to say about her work methods:

'I practice Vibrational Medicine and I have devised my own diagnostic test combining two methods of dowsing I learned from America and here in England. Dowsing is a clever way of asking our subconscious what is wrong with our bodies. This may sound strange, but our body knows how to heal itself when injured. For example, if we cut ourselves, our body heals it in its own time and correctly;

something we humans take for granted and for which we do not give our bodies credit. We think we know better and can do quicker. You cannot push the body to heal faster, as much as it is inconvenient to our busy lives. There is a consequence for doing this since cells are designed to work at their own speed. The brain is divided into two, the conscious and subconscious. The subconscious deals with the automatic nervous system, things we do not have to think about such as breathing, swallowing, blinking, keeping the heart going and fighting infections and diseases.This is the part that I access with dowsing. All the answers are there stored like a computer, and each person's body has its own history and allergies and chemical makeup.

Once I find the underlying problem or imbalance, I treat the cause using magnetized water or pillules giving help to the body. The human or animal cell takes that energy in thirty seconds. Many people feel better before leaving the clinic, but being negative in attitude will drain the energy and the client may need many more treatments. The condition may need several sessions to treat because there is only so much the body can do, in a short time, by itself. It can only heal at its own pace. It is like peeling the layers of an onion. Over twenty years I have witnessed that a pattern was occurring and I discovered that everyone had similar problems because of medicines used daily, even toothpaste! Over the years I discovered what chemicals do to people's bodies.'

Brian had been using a powder-coating spraying system to coat the beds and furniture produced in the forge, for many months prior to becoming unwell. A later inspection showed a fault in the ventilation system. Brian had 'shot himself in the leg' and he was fighting for his life.

What was more frightening was that when he eventually saw the hospital Specialist and told him all that had happened, the Specialist refused to listen to him, saying he was not interested and that he considered Brian had advanced cancer. A scan had shown a mass in his abdomen. We knew this was most likely chronic inflammation and a build up of the polyester resin, which solidifies in the gut and is notorious for causing intestinal blockages.

We walked out the hospital disappointed and frustrated at not being heard. The failure of the Specialist to even consider our suspicions then resulted in a protracted complaint procedure with the hospital authorities. We had lost faith in the medical profession, that had rejected our experiences, and our suspicions, and who wanted us both to adopt their blinkered vision to the situation. It was a very terrifying experience having to trust in our own knowing, when Brian's life was on the line.

Meanwhile Brian was being treated by Uta, who was flushing his system of the toxic substance and at the same he took many natural body-cleansing products. By August of 2009 there was a marked improvement; so much so, that we took a holiday abroad. By this time he was eating quite well again, so he returned to his GP and asked him to seek out a Specialist in Industrial Medicine. The GP examined Brian and said he could not feel any growth and said he did not look as though he had cancer. For weeks the GP attempted to find a Specialist but with no success. All such Specialists said they were too busy to see Brian, even privately! However, by October, a sizeable swelling began to show in Brian's abdomen and he was starting to feel very unwell again.

Uta said the polyester resin had begun to irritate and fuse with an old injury in Brian's stomach, that he had sustained many years earlier, from heavy lifting during his occupation as a landscape gardener. The combination of a bleed in the old injury and the resin was a dangerous mix and a sizeable growth was forming and was beginning to mutate.

Brian returned to the hospital and two further Specialists told him he had an inoperable cancerous tumour of the abdomen and that he had only a short time left to live. We could not believe the verdict and I just seemed to know that we would receive another phone call from the hospital within days of being told Brian's growth was inoperable. That call did arrive, from a Specialist Surgeon we had never met before. He said he had been at a Team Meeting with his colleagues during which patients' cases were discussed and that he did not agree with his colleagues that Brian's growth was inoperable. He asked us to meet with him the following day. He still painted a grave picture, saying that without surgery, Brian had very little time left to live. However, he said, he was a Craftsman, not a Scientist. He said he expected rampant cancer and that he might just have to open Brian up and investigate and then stitch him back up again if the tumour had spread extensively. However, he felt it might just be possible for him to cut out the growth, although he expected malignant cells to have travelled everywhere throughout Brian's body. We spent some time that day with this Surgeon and it all felt surreal. He was so likeable, easy to talk with and extremely relational, very interested in us as people and he felt like an old friend. He told us that before he operated he wanted to get to know what kind of person Brian was and to understand how he ticked. We just seemed to know he would be successful and that his prognosis for Brian was wrong. As we left his company that day, he asked Brian if he was as confident on the inside as he appeared upon the outside. The answer for Brian and me was 'absolutely'. Uta told Brian that he had saved the life of this Surgeon, who was about to operate upon him, in a previous life!

Within a few days Brian was operated on. He was in surgery for many hours. At the end of the day the Surgeon returned to Brian's bedside smiling from ear to ear. He said he had completely removed a 118mm x 87mm tumour and found no spread in the immediate area. It would take ten days for the pathology report to confirm this, but he suspected an aggressive type of cancer.

Whilst Brian was in the operating theatre, I had a text message from a friend and colleague of mine, who rescued and rehabilitated race horses. Our friendship evolved from our mutual love of horses and we had never discussed anything remotely connected to healing or other spiritual matters. I was, therefore, very surprised when her text message gave the strange name of somebody she said was over-seeing Brian's operation. I remarked to her, at a later date, that the name she gave us sounded like that of an 'Extra-Terrestrial Being'. Shocked that I had come to that conclusion, she admitted it was such a being that was helping Brian.

What was so evidential for us was that Brian had been receiving, for several weeks prior to surgery, healing from extra-terrestrials via a contact our son had made in the USA on one of his travels. We had decided to seek their help because Brian was critically ill and we knew it was going to take some kind of miracle if he was going to pull through. We trusted and believed that the ETs had that off-planet potential. In fact the ETs had agreed to watch over and intervene in his surgery, to aid its complete success. We were well aware that Extra-Terrestrials are able to utilize amazing therapeutic interventions in a totally non-invasive manner. We had also come to understand and appreciate, from our own studies in recent years, that the ETs' perceptions of the psychological processes that had caused the physical illnesses to manifest in the first place were extremely profound and illuminating. There was absolutely no way this friend of mine had any knowledge of the help Brian was receiving. Just the sort of evidence we expect these days.

I am aware that I have invited my reader to take a huge leap in possible perception here by introducing this content relating to Extra Terrestrials. However, as I have suggested before in previous chapters when I have briefly detailed our interactions with extremely complex matters, charity is called for here, yet again. Maybe I can suggest that my readers might like to look into Extra Terrestrial interactions with our planet. There is much documented material available to us these days.

Ten days later the Surgeon came to Brian's bedside, yet again grinning from ear to ear. He threw the pathology report onto the bed and said he could not believe what he was reading. Malignancy was minor, with absolutely no spread beyond the immediate tumour, although the Surgeon felt there would be some malignant cells in his vascular system.

We know that cancer is a word for the layman. Malignancy is the term used by the medical profession to define defective cells. The Vibropath, Uta, had said Brian had mild malignancy developing, but that the growth was in fact full of polyester resin that had mixed with blood and this was beginning to form a life of its own, thus the need for its urgent removal. The Surgeon had said that a tumour of the size he had removed had to have been growing for many years, but this clearly was not the case.

Brian was given the choice to have CheMotherapy after surgery, which is standard practice in the NHS. He declined, much to the disbelief of the Oncology Department. Instead of choosing to allow more poisonous chemicals into his body, he opted instead to take a natural, rejuvenating and naturopathic approach to his recovery, having already experienced the ravages to his body caused by the polyester resin, that his Vibropath, Uta advised him was equivalent to two concurrent administrations of CheMotherapy.

Brian returned home on the 20th November 2009 and within four months he had put back on the four-and-a-half stones in weight that he had lost during the past twelve months. He began to look years younger and fitter than he had for a very long time. He returned at six months to the hospital for a check up and was given a scan. The results showed nothing abnormal and all the medical staff were amazed at his recovery, the quality of his blood readings and his weight gain in such a short time. They asked us what treatment he had been undergoing! We told them his rapid recovery was the result, not only of treatment by Uta, the Vibropath, to drive out the side-effects of the surgery and drug intake, but also the nutritional guidance he had received from another energy therapist, who incidentally happened to be Pam, the same therapist who had worked with Danny-Boy and myself a few years prior. Pam had worked with many people suffering from serious illness over the years and had assisted their complete return to health. One member of the hospital staff suggested we write a report on how the transformation had occurred. To us it just felt like a miracle, for which we were very grateful. Between us all we had defied death.

Many of our friends who were healers had also helped Brian through the difficult months. Their combined projected healing energies were directed to Brian on the day of his surgery. John-Luke, my ex-tutor, now living in Canada and practising as a Teaching

Shaman, together with several of his Apprentices, had been using the time of the Fire Ceremony to call for Brian's healing at the time of his surgery.

Just after surgery, Brian was sent a pastel sketch of the Extra Terrestrial, who my friend had advised was with him on the day of his operation. His name was Zeras. The sketch came via the daughter of a medium and psychic artist who had left this world some years prior. She had sketched ET contacts for people when she was alive but had also left behind sketches of ETs who would be working in

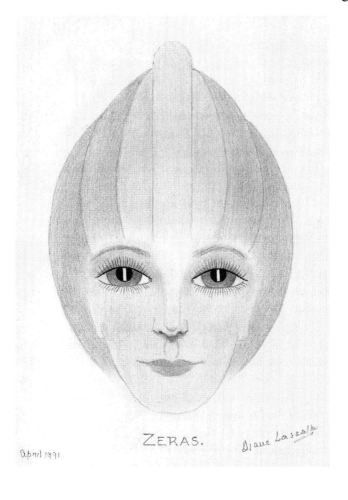

ZERAS.   Diane Lascelle

April 1991

the future with people. Brian, a few months after surgery, began to call on the help of this ET to assist others who began to approach him for help. For several years prior, Brian had been working at distant healing on people and animals. Like his ability to dowse for lost animals and items, he was effective as a channel for distant healing. Now he had another helper, this time of the ET variety. There are many Extra Terrestrial beings wanting and willing to help the human race, but as with Yesterday's People of the human race, they cannot interfere with our free will and the help has to be invited.

A further six months down the line, just twelve months after his major surgery, Brian returned again for a hospital check. There was genuine amazement on the faces of the medical staff who had seen him just a year prior, when he was so near to death. Instead of asking him to return every six months, as is required in a five year recovery plan, they offered him a once a year follow up if he felt he needed it. They knew he was on an alternative programme and we told them that his therapists were medical dowsers and they had confirmed that there was not one malignant cell left in his body. This piece of information was recorded on Brian's medical records. We felt that more attention was paid to our opinion this time, and that maybe a small chink had been made in the armour of the NHS.

There is little doubt that without the intervention of that brave Surgeon, Brian would have lost his life. Having now worked myself in Complementary Therapy for seven years, I felt that, at long last, there was hope for a fusion some day between orthodox medicine and the numerous complementary therapies available. The alternative route is not for everybody. Some people are happy to place responsibility for their health in the hands of others, whom they consider to be more expert at it than them. However, for those who have the courage to consider taking a degree of responsibility for themselves, a combination of the two opposites is a wonderful possibility – the two worlds beginning to work together.

As well as the healing by Extra-Terrestrials, who had worked to rebuild Brian's system on an etheric level in the latter stages of his deteriorating health, he embarked upon a course of Psychospiritual

Counselling with a remarkable lady, who helped him understand his lifetime pattern of giving everything of himself in service to others. In early childhood he had developed this habit, as a defence and survival mechanism, but now it was not in his best interests and prevented him from being the person he was meant to be. Brian had always been 'a rescuer'. When we are children, particularly in the early years of life, relationship patterns develop, mirrored to us by parents and carers. Not all children are fortunate enough to receive authentic mirroring and so develop survival personalities. These are carried into adult life and can make life very uncomfortable and unfulfilling. My description of the process of Psychosynthesis in Chapter Twenty-Seven relates to this phenomenon.

Brian is now a very different person as a result; still kind, generous and loving but with boundaries and self-respect firmly in place. Psychospiritually speaking, it is said that a person may have to die psychologically in order to be reborn emotionally as the person they were meant to be. Brian, it would appear, went a bit further and almost died physically as well! What in fact this emotional death relates to is the re-birth/re-synthesis of the psyche resulting from personal in-depth therapeutic work unravelling the persona and freeing up the spirit to allow authenticity to return. This is where the work of the Psychospiritual Counsellor comes into play, as mentioned in Chapter Twenty-Seven, to hold the sacred space for the client to find that authenticity.

Daily life after such a near-death experience takes on a totally different colour. Every day becomes a gift. It concerns both of us that some areas of the medical system appears to us to be extremely fear-based and negative. Tell a person they are going to die and they will. The power of auto-suggestion is great; why else is it used so much in the practice of hypnotherapy? Brian and I saw several hospital patients surrendering their will to those they considered to know more about their patients than the patients knew about themselves. What concerns us is the encouraged surrender of the patients to the outcome opinions of their medical carers. One young female Registrar, attempting to understand a scan of Brian's stomach prior to surgery, actually said that it looked as if he already had secondary tumours in his lungs, voicing her grave concerns that things did not look good for Brian's long-term future. Brian's Surgeon later dismissed this statement as an incorrect opinion. Given to a vulnerable patient, such an ill-considered verdict could have been a self-fulfilling death sentence. Fortunately, neither of us was prepared to accept her prognosis.

It seems the average NHS view places very little emphasis on the ability of the human will to overcome adversity. In our European culture, we are not sufficiently educated or encouraged to know and believe in ourselves. Miracles are the domain of God, so salvation is in his hands, not our own. This is powerfully reminiscent and a legacy of the Catholic Inquisition of the Cathars during the thirteenth century in Europe as mentioned in the Epilogue to this book. The Cathars knew they were immortal beings and they understood their individual potential. They also had a great understanding of Nature's plants and their ability to heal human and animal life. However, the Catholic Church then, and many other branches of the Anglican Church since, considers such opinion blasphemous. I have met people who consider that what I write about is blasphemous and in these apparently advanced times, this attitude I see to be a threat to our survival on this planet.

CONCLUSION – JUNE 2011

We are fast approaching 2012. I see a world on the cusp of great change, with many positive indicators that receive very little mass publicity. Brian and I, and many others like us, have now served long and challenging apprenticeships in this lifetime and we know that, deep inside each and every one of us, there is great untapped potential. It is just that some of us have not been encouraged to 'wake up'.

For sure, it is clear to us all to see, this planet is crying out. Many, many of earth's inhabitants are living in abject poverty, whilst others live in material excess and the natural environment is struggling. Greed, neglect and abuse – our planet suffers from the same angst that the human race mirrors. Many dire warnings are out in circulation, relating to the approach of 2012 and they are not without substance. Fear and conflict are the emotions that maintain this status quo.

Today we have forgotten who we really are, who we can be and what we can jointly achieve. We need to heal our psyches and uncover the true human spirit and potential that lies within us all, buried after centuries of misinformation, indoctrination and loss of connection to the creative life force. If we can rescue ourselves, by profound psychological healing, we can begin to shine once more and in so doing, our planet will begin to mirror the same transformation.

Many of earth's inhabitants have to live in survival mode – damaged by their upbringing and desensitized by their cultural persuasions. The planet is financially, morally and emotionally bankrupt and almost, but not completely, spiritually bankrupt. It is this tiny light of spiritual possibility – that small flame that burns within us all – that is the key to possible transformation of ourselves and this planet, if we so choose.

This, for me, is what 2012 is all about – personal choice – for that is the commodity that many of us have allowed to be erased from our belief system. We have become so desensitized by those we have delegated our power and decisions to, that we believe we are now helpless as individuals – but I know it is not so. We need, both individually and collectively, to wake up. We are in this mire together. If we can remember what and who we really are, then we can realise our potential as humans and the planet may survive. We have the choice!

As I write this conclusion possibilities are beginning to show themselves to Brian and me. We are beginning to learn more about the Medieval Site upon which we have been living for the past five years with our extended family. It has been very obvious to us all living here that the site has seen some pretty dark history. For all of us, being sensitive, the negative energy has resulted in repercussions yet again for family life, as it did upon the previous site we had all lived upon with the history of a Civil War massacre. Such sites can evoke energetically a form of re-enactment. We have from time to time called upon outsiders to help us understand and clear the karma of the site, but the process is always ongoing as we move through layer upon layer of historic energetic imprint.

Just a few people, living in the same village, who are themselves sensitive to energetics, have spoken with us about the negativity that can be felt upon this ancient land and they too have made their own contributions to its clearance. Our farm sits close to the site of an ancient monastery and we know that the land has been used for religious purposes. Many psychically gifted people over the years, who have not known where I actually live, have told me that I am upon a site with a somewhat traumatic history, with the remains of people murdered a very long time ago. During the last couple of years, I have worked regularly at trying to seek help from the other worlds to cleanse and heal the wounds of these ancient lands.

I still need reassurance from time to time about the accuracy of my internal observations and at one stage I wrote to Mary Kingston, the medium who is mentioned several times in this book and who possesses great skills at reading the past. Mary had never visited the site and I had given her no knowledge about it whatsoever. I just asked her to see what she could pick up about the site and the surrounding area. I wanted to test my own observations and the mental question I put out was that I wanted confirmation of a tunnel running from our farmland to the valley below that had been the site of the ancient monastery. The first piece of information Mary offered me was that there was a tunnel. She then went on to confirm many of the visions I had seen and to elaborate considerably upon the multi-layered history of the site, which had seen so much strife, hardship, death and oppression. Village events during the years we have been living here have certainly mirrored to some extent unrest. This is what I am speaking about when I talk of sites exhibiting re-enactment. Mary's visions of the past involved foreign Monks coming into the Monastery and not being welcomed by the local population.

I have mentioned previously the fact that I would call upon the etheric herd of Celtic horses that Brian and I invited to the valley here when we left our previous home set on Celtic land. It was that herd I called upon, in true Shamanic practice, to help release the souls of those trapped within a time warp and whose energies could affect those living on the land today. Shamanic practice was something I had been feeling myself drawing towards and comfortable with in more recent years. I find ancient Shamanic rituals familiar to a part of me. They offer me tools and practices that give me protection and a framework to work in effortless and fluid fusion with the holographic layers of being. I suspect such practice was just buried deep within my soul memory. I had probably worked in this way many centuries prior.

Our increasing materialistic culture has allowed us to become alienated from the natural world and yet many today seek to re-kindle this relationship by engaging with Shamanic practice, to find their way back to inner harmony. Shamanism is the oldest form of personal development and revolves around connection to nature, allowing an opening up of the gateways to other dimensions of being. It is this underlying thread of connection to the natural worlds that links the myriad of Shamanistic cultures of the world. All races have their own roots in Shamanic culture and ritual and for us today, it is about finding our individual ways back to the practices that resonate within.

We were also aware that there were powerful ley lines running through the land that were contaminated with the negativity of times past. We managed to heal much of the historical damage by placing crystals and other mechanical processes to help pull positive energy transmission into these energy lines.

Brian and I are now, yet again, saying – What Next? We feel our work is completed here and that it is time to move on.

I end my story with the wonderful fact that I believe it is quite possible that I have found The Rev. William Thomas reincarnated back onto the same estate in Dorset, where he served as a Cleric four hundred years ago. One day I put a question out into infinity: 'William Thomas where are you, is a part of you leading an earth life now, can I find you or will you make your way to me one day? Within weeks, a series of unlikely events brought about my meeting with a man, whom I eventually came to intuit as the possible reincarnation of William Thomas, now Napier Marten of Crichel. It happened like this.

Brian has a fascination for powerful motor engines and had spread the word among his friends that he had a Specialist V8 Diesel engine fitted to a vehicle he wanted to sell. Several months later Brian received a phone from a man saying he was interested in buying the vehicle, giving his name as Mr. Martin. Within a couple of days he came to our home and gave a Christian name of Napier. Napier seemed an interesting and unusual man. We spoke generalities and we asked each other about our working lives, whereupon Napier told me he was a Craniosacral Therapist. I immediately responded that The Craniosacral Therapy Association was one of the organisations I had been the Administrator for a few years prior to becoming a Counsellor and running Body Mind Spirit in Dorset. We all chatted comfortably for some time and as Napier left I asked him for his contact details as I thought I might be able to find him some clients. As I looked at the card he gave to me I saw his surname was spelt with an 'e' – Marten. So this man was Napier Marten. I rapidly put two and two together. Marten was the surname of the long-established family in residence at Crichel and I knew that the name Napier was also connected to his ancestral family line. At that stage I just thought the coincidence a little strange, but thought no more of it.

Within a couple of weeks Napier returned, with a friend who wanted to see the vehicle, as he would be involved in its restoration work. Again we chatted easily on many subjects other than the engine. As Napier went to leave and he stepped down from the front door step and our eyes met at the same height (Napier is a tall man and I am quite short) I felt a shock of recognition, a spark of connection come to me from his eyes and a question immediately hit my mind – was this, could this be, William Thomas?

To elaborate, my understanding is that we all posses an oversoul and it is but a fragment of this that reincarnates, the purpose being to grow through experience and feed enhanced understanding back to the oversoul.

Napier actually returned several times to visit, saying he felt somewhat drawn to both of us. I decided eventually I would tell him at one of these meet ups that I was aware of his roots at Crichel and that I had met with his Mother, The Hon. Mary Anna Marten, several years prior, when seeking her approval to mention the estate in my first autobiography. He was intrigued and I offered him a copy of my book. At this stage I did not let him know anything of my suspicions that he might be a reincarnation of William Thomas.

Napier came to supper one evening, having read my story and over a few glasses of wine he looked across the table at me and asked:

'Do you think I was William Thomas?' I was reluctant to commit myself, but he went on to mention that it felt somewhat strangely possible as it had occurred to him many times in his earlier life that he might consider taking Holy Orders. This revelation encouraged me to admit my suspicions, but I hastened to add that although it felt possible to me, I did not want him to just trust my intuition. It would have to feel completely right to him. However, Napier did not strike me as the kind of person who would accept another person's interpretation of anything. He was too much his own man.

I have already mentioned how people can sometimes react to the influences of historical past events that may have occurred in the close proximity, to where they find themselves in the present. Locations, and people for that matter, can sometimes manifest, or hint at in some other way, events from times long past. Napier told us how he had been estranged from his family and had been disinherited because of his family breakup and other issues. He had spent many years travelling, meeting with indigenous peoples and searching, I suspect, for a degree of purpose, during the course of which he had undertaken much work for the benefit of the Cetaceans (Whales, Dolphins etc.) seeking to protect them from Sonar violations in the oceans of the world.

Napier's estrangement and disinheritance felt to me like an historical re-enactment, a replay of some long past drama on the site at Crichel. William Thomas some four hundred years prior had fought Sir Henry Uvedale bitterly in Queen Elizabeth's Courts over the unfairness of the estate Tithe Apportionments, and had left the estate. Napier had fallen out with his family over, amongst other things, the running of the estate, and left. Brian told Napier he would return to Crichel one day and that his family would once again include him. Napier's Mother died only a few years later and Brian's prediction came to pass. For me, the reunion with Napier brings a sense of peace and joy and innate remembrance of the continuity of our soul life.

Here is how Napier experienced that meeting of old friends:

'There is a particular swirl around the solar plexus, often accompanied by goose bumps up the left arm, when there is a meeting of truth and the confluence of those who have shared parallel experiences. Such meetings may also exhibit a near overwhelming desire to tell everything one has ever known, felt or done to the other in a trice, yet feeling zero words are needed as everything is already known between the parties. I felt thus when I met Josephine.

A friend had been looking for a particular vehicle for me and after sometime he rang to say a vehicle that fitted my bill was for sale in Somerset. After much badgering I finally extracted the telephone number of the seller from my friend and we set off to meet the appointment. The first striking moment of the journey was the turning down a small road which immediately took us into a different older rural scene than the one we had just left 100 yards behind us, more so because for many years I had passed this little turning and knew one day I would need to explore this backwater to find someone or something.

On a cold clear day as I recall, we were met by a view of outstanding beauty across the whole of the Blackmoor Vale, the image of Tess milking on the summer dawns was vivid, the memory of Elms and years of steady country life with all its rigour and hard-ship was contained in the instant. I felt this was a powerful place and to be respected.

We looked at the vehicle, ideal, I bought it and soon realised it was more the vehicle of my meeting with Josephine and Brian than the hard metal itself. I had met friends in the collective consciousness and I assured them I would love to come and see them again when time was more at ease with us. For in this brief encounter we discovered a common interest in Complimentary Medicine, engineer-ing, trees, the way of the world and the way of other realms, and perhaps most intriguing, Josephine had met my Mother many years before while researching her book. The shock of recognition Josephine writes about in her words was as strong for me too.

I forget the exact chronology of visits; the first time I did Craniosacral work with Josephine we journeyed well beyond the norm, both of us charged by the energy exchanged in the session. I also forget upon which visit Josephine gave me her book, which I shelved for a while to await the moment it felt right to delve into its pages. It is a personal rollercoaster and gives the reader a front seat in its theatre of the bizarre and remarkable.

When I read the name William Thomas I had that aforementioned swirl very deep within, the more intense because the recognition was across centuries. I avoided questioning the meaning; I sat in the rightness of it and was eager to ask Josephine at the earliest opportunity, with some trepidation, if this was her reading of the matter. If this is the way of the Universe, so be it: I am moved by the naturalness of this experience, the ease and the lack of need to explain or find reasons to explore deeper; it is about the oneness of things and the recognition of this is all that is required of us. By so doing we are fulfilling our purpose. I feel this to be true because it is all so simple, for Simplicity is the Universe's greatest dream.'

As I was coming to the end of writing this story, I visited an extremely talented tarot card reader in Bournemouth, Donna White, whose reputation is well know. Donna told me that my previous autobiography, published originally some twenty years ago, documented experiences and activities that were 'ahead of their time', being offered to a public not yet ready for new time dimensions. Now, however, the public were more sympathetic to new realities and that, hopefully, my writings presented now to a more enlightened world. Within a few months I went on to meet a Publisher, specialising in Transpersonal material, who expressed interest in re-presenting my story. My journey and training in Psychology at the Sacred Space Institute and my meeting John-Luke Edwards, my Tutor, had allowed me to pull my Parallel

Worlds together and make some sense of my life. Now, thanks to Ian Thorp at Archive Publishing, I offer my readers a Transpersonal Autobiography.

Not for the first time in my story, a series of significant and meaningful encounters with others had occurred, prompting me further along life's pathway, maybe giving me just a hint that life may involve a sense of mission or pre-planning. In my early school days, I had felt that sense of purpose and mission (Introduction). Hopefully these synchronistic pointers will continue to occur during the coming years, allowing me to feel a sense of completion when I eventually leave this world this time around.

EPILOGUE

The Gnostic Christian perception of sin was somewhat more subtle than the orthodox version and contained but one principle – that ignorance was sinful. Of course the ignorance referred to was not the ignorance of the classroom, but ignorance of that which is available to all of us, namely knowledge of who, what and where we are, knowledge of ourselves – hence their name 'The Gnostics'. It is not difficult to appreciate their next conclusion, that ignorance leads to fear and there lies the rub, for fearful people are forever seeking security and certainty and will gladly follow the flag of any articulate scoundrel who will promise them just that.

A widespread Christian culture of the middle ages, the Albigensian or Cathar Christians, were particularly conscious that the penalty for ignorance was the ease with which those in power could bend the energies and enthusiasms of the people to their own advantage, and for this reason the exercise of 'power' became, within their ethics, not only undesirable but immoral. To keep the abuse of power under control it was necessary that each individual member of the society should be kept in constant awareness of his own worth, his own power, and his own ability to withstand the influences and temptations of others. It is astonishing to record how many of the nobility of Southern Europe subscribed to this philosophy but, sadly, the most powerful section of the establishment, namely the church, was entirely hostile to the whole idea, for in the face of such individualism it was apparent that Authority would hold little sway, and the power of orthodoxy rests upon Authority. And so the Inquisition was invented and an entire culture was annihilated, nobility and all, to the tune of many tens of thousands of lives in a vicious and shameless crusade which has been conveniently omitted from the history books. By such means are belief patterns and habits maintained.

Today the intuition of the individual still awaits liberation from the abuse of power. The establishment that wields it is not an organised body, neither is it a conspiracy as such. The nearest, I think, that we can get to a description is to perceive it as a layer of society which has a corporate interest in maintaining power. It contains certain institutions whose interest; which range through the manipulation of money, genes and belief systems, are cloaked by a veneer of Authority which, when scratched, all too frequently reveals a mishmash of human frailty and pseudo-intellectualism spiced with greed.

In this book Josephine Sellers has described her own brush with Authority, and the perceptive reader will note how from an early age she had to struggle against it in order to establish her own integrity.

John Lloyd, (rtd Maj. Royal Marines)
Retired Schoolmaster
Researcher

Lightning Source UK Ltd.
Milton Keynes UK
UKOW050909301111

182924UK00001B/2/P